IT Services Organization

IT Infrastructure Library

Andy McDonnell

LONDON: The Stationery Office

CCTA
Central Computer and Telecommunications Agency

Sixth impression 2000

ISBN   0 11 330563 X

ISSN   0956 2591

This is one of the books published in the IT
Infrastructure Library series.

For further information on CCTA products,
contact:

CCTA Library,
Rosebery Court,
St Andrews Business Park
NORWICH NR7 0HS.
Telephone 01603 704930
GTN 3040 4930

ITIL ® is a registered trademark of CCTA

This document has been produced using
procedures conforming to
BS 5750 Part 1: 1987; ISO 9001: 1987.

Table of contents

Foreword

Welcome to the IT Infrastructure Library module on **IT Services Organization.**

In their respective areas the IT Infrastructure Library publications complement and provide more detail than the IS Guides.

The ethos behind the development of the IT Infrastructure Library is the recognition that organizations are becoming increasingly dependent on IT in order to satisfy their corporate aims and meet their business needs. This growing dependency leads to growing requirement for quality IT services. In this context quality means 'matched to business needs and user requirements as these evolve'.

This module is one of a series of codes of practice intended to facilitate the quality management of IT services and of the IT Infrastructure. (By IT Infrastructure, we mean organizations' computers and networks - hardware, software and computer related communications, upon which application systems and IT services are built and run). The codes of practice will assist organizations to provide quality IT services in the face of skill shortages, system complexity, rapid change, growing user expectations, current and future user requirements.

Underpinning the IT Infrastructure is the Environmental Infrastructure upon which it is built. Environmental topics are covered in separate sets of guides within the IT Infrastructure Library.

IT service management is a complex subject which for presentational and practical reasons has been broken down within the IT Infrastructure Library into a series of modules. A complete list of current and planned modules is available from the CCTA IT Infrastructure Management Services at the address given at the back of this module.

Consistency versus new challenges

The IT Infrastructure Library has been produced over a period of five years during which there have been significant changes in the business environment of Central Government. Major initiatives such as Next Steps, Citizen's Charter and Competing for Quality are affecting the organization of Departments and the way in which they conduct their business. These changes are having a significant effect on the IT Directorate.

The production of later volumes of the IT Infrastructure Library has therefore presented the dual challenges of maintaining consistency with earlier publications while ensuring relevance to today's Government departments. Both the changes in the Government department business environment and latest thinking in IT service management need to be taken into account. For example, the impact of market testing is addressed in the later books, even though the Competing for Quality White Paper had not been issued when the early books were published.

Some of the challenges which IT service suppliers face are:

* meeting requirements specified by the customer

* improved timeliness of response to customer needs

* cutting costs to provide economic, competitively priced services

* a clear separation of supply (provider of services) and demand (customer of services) with defined interfaces, regardless of whether or not the supply is in-house

* devolution of authority and budgets enabling the customer to decide which IT service suppliers to use.

Many of these issues have been identified and addressed in earlier volumes of the IT Infrastructure Library. However, changes in the business environment have provided new focus and emphasis which is particularly evident in this and other recent volumes. Further information is available in CCTA's Market Testing IS/IT publications.

Common themes and relationships in the IT Infrastructure Library

Three closely related modules in the Managers' Set of the IT Infrastructure Library provide additional information about common themes which run through all other modules in the Library: IT Services Organization, Planning and Control for IT Services and Quality Management for IT Services. These books give three different viewpoints or ways of looking at the IT Services organization:

* **IT Services Organization** concentrates on organizational structure, describes roles, skills and experience required by people, and provides a framework for reviewing the organizational structure to meet changing circumstances

* **Planning and Control for IT Services** covers information flows and the development of an appropriate planning and control system to meet the requirements of the organization; people are one of the resources to be considered and the organizational structure will influence information flows, but the module has a wider focus covering all aspects of planning and control

* **Quality Management for IT Services** is concerned with putting in place an ISO9001 conformant quality management system; it encompasses organizational and planning and control aspects, since they are covered by the ISO9001 standard, but refers to the above two modules rather than repeating information.

In general, the three modules answer the following questions:

* who and where?

  - IT Services Organization

* what and when?

  - Planning and Control for IT Services

* what, why and how?

  - Quality Management for IT Services.

The three modules address distinct but closely related aspects of IT service management. Organizations using the IT Infrastructure Library may choose to use the three modules as part of a coordinated project. In particular, changes to organizational structure and the development of planning and control processes will often need to be considered in parallel. In addition, many organizations seek to develop procedures in line with the ISO9001 quality management standard which covers organizational issues and the use of plans and controls, but has a wider scope and refers to policies and standards, detailed procedures, agreements with the customer and document control.

The close links between the subject matters of these three modules, and indeed with others in the Library, means that there is a degree of overlap. Nevertheless these three modules present different but valid viewpoints of managing IT Services.

The structure of the module is, in essence:

* a **Management summary** aimed at senior managers (Directors of IT and above, typically down to Civil Service Grade 5), senior IT staff and, in some cases, users or office managers (typically Civil Service Grades 5 to 7)

* the main body of the text, aimed at IT middle management (typically grades 7 to HEO)

* technical detail in Annexes.

The module gives the main **guidance** in sections 3 to 5; explains the **benefits, costs and possible problems** in section 6, which may be of interest to senior staff; and provides information on **tools** (requirements and examples of real-life availability) in section 7.

CCTA is working with the IT industry to foster the development of software tools to underpin the guidance contained within the codes of practice (ie to make adherence to the module more practicable), and ultimately to automate functions.

If you have any comments on this or other modules, do please let us know. A **Comments sheet** is provided with every module. Alternatively you may wish to contact us directly using the reference point given in **Further information**.

Thank you. We hope you find this module useful.

Acknowledgement

The assistance of the following contributors is gratefully acknowledged:

David Paget and Gareth Bunn (under contract to CCTA from Ernst & Young Management Consultants)

Peter Hyde, management and training consultant (under contract to CCTA).

1. Management summary

1.1 Background

Recent government initiatives such as the Competing for Quality White Paper and the Citizen's Charter make clear the paramount importance of quality and customer satisfaction in the provision of public services.

The same principles apply for the provision of IT services. In the past, internal IT providers have sometimes been seen as inward looking and focused on technology, rather than on the requirements of customers. Whether this has always been justified or not, it is clear that IT providers must adopt processes, practices and an organizational structure which will deliver the services their customers want.

The current organizational structures of in-house providers of IT services have often evolved over several years. Changing demands from customers, the need to contain costs, to improve services, to be more business-like and, increasingly, the need to compete with external companies during **market testing**, mean IT Directorates must look critically at their existing organizational structures, and ensure they remain appropriate.

The organizational structure adopted by an IT Directorate depends on its particular circumstances but, in general, the management team for the IT Directorate will include:

* the IT Director - who is head of the IT Directorate

* heads of groups responsible for the IT Directorate's main business services (such as applications development and maintenance)

* head of finance

* head of marketing and sales.

IT Directorates may provide various types of service:

* operational services - continuous or regular delivery of services such as access to applications and data, operating computer systems and maintaining networks, and associated customer support facilities

* project services - such as applications software development

* planning services - such as advice and guidance on development of IS strategies.

In all cases the required service should be agreed with customers and documented in Service Level Agreements or similar formal agreements.

This module is concerned with operational IT services and throughout the module, the term *IT service* will have this meaning.

The delivery and management of operational IT services, and management of the IT infrastructure on which those services are run are referred to collectively as *service management*. The organizational group responsible for service management is the *IT Services Organization*.

The module outlines functions, management roles and structures for the IT Services Organization, and provides a framework for an organizational review and change programme. It should be borne in mind that in many cases organizational reviews will have a wider scope than the IT Services Organization alone, but the scope of this module is in keeping with that of the IT Infrastructure Library of which it is a component.

1.2   Key messages

Key messages of the module are:

*   organizational design must seek to enable the organization to meets its objectives and the demands of the business environment in which it operates; since both objectives and environment vary there can be no universal organizational solution for all situations

*   service management is a sufficiently coherent and important component of most IT Directorates to be considered as a discrete organizational grouping - the IT Services Organization

*   the IT Services Organization must be seen in the context of the way IS provision is approached in the parent organization as a whole; three main approaches can be identified - centralized, decentralized and a federal model which combines centralized and decentralized elements

*   the IT Services Organization must also be considered in relation to the structure of the wider IT Directorate; it is at this level that the overall customer interface is likely to be determined and the need for interfaces within the IT Directorate can be identified

* organizational design should be approached from the customer's perspective; the focus should be on facilitating the delivery of services which meet customer requirements (which should be set out in Service Level Agreements) and on simplifying communications with customers

* the IT Services Organization should be constantly monitoring its business environment for trends and changes to which it needs to respond; major changes in the business environment will often trigger formal organizational review projects

* the IT Services Organization must aim to ensure that it is sufficiently flexible to be able to respond to changes in requirements, themselves dictated by business needs, quickly and successfully

* organizational culture should be oriented towards customers and the delivery of services, with technology seen as a means to this end, rather than an end in itself

* the implementation of a new organizational structure must be understood as a management of change process and requires careful planning and management.

2. Introduction

2.1 Purpose

The purpose of this module is to help IT Services Managers find the best way of structuring their organization in order to deliver quality IT services.

The module provides an approach to reviewing the IT Services Organization and a framework for organizational change. The underlying principles of the approach described will also be appropriate when creating a new IT Services Organization.

The module provides generic guidance. It does not set out to define a single solution appropriate to every organization. While there is no universal organizational solution, the module raises many common issues which an IT Directorate might face when reviewing the IT Services Organization.

2.2 Target readership

This module is aimed primarily at IT Services Managers. It is also relevant to IT Directors and other IT managers who may be involved in the establishment or re-structuring of the IT Services Organization. It is assumed that, whatever or whoever motivates the review, the main responsibility for the review project and any resulting changes to the IT Services Organization will rest with the IT Services Manager.

Some of the material contained within the module will also be useful to personnel managers and reviewers such as staff inspectors who may be involved in identifying the need for, and organization of, service management functions.

2.3 Scope

The main focus of this module is IT service management - the activities, roles and responsibilities involved in planning and managing the delivery of operational IT services.

Service management is taken to be the responsibility of the IT Services Organization, part of the IT Directorate, which acts as the central provider of operational IT services to internal customers (this might involve the control of some subcontracted services).

The range of functions carried out by the IT Services Organization is indicated in section 3.0.4, with a brief description of service management functions covered in the IT Infrastructure Library given in Annex B.

The organization of software development and maintenance groups, responsibilities for the development of technical policies and standards, and long term infrastructure planning are beyond the direct scope of this module. Nevertheless, in some cases the IT Services Organization will have responsibility for (and in most cases an input to) these activities.

Within the module, the term *parent organization* is used for the wider business organization (for example a government department) of which the IT Directorate is a part, along with the various business areas which are its customers. Other parts of the IT Directorate including software development and maintenance teams may also be customers of the IT Services Organization.

The guidance covers:

* the need to consider the IT Services Organization in the context of the wider business environment, organizational trends and pressures

* how IT service management functions can be drawn together in a logical manner

* interfaces which should be established between IT Services and the rest of the IT Directorate, and the customer community

* definitions of functions and roles for the key management positions in IT Services.

This module is generally concerned with reviews of the IT Services Organization as a whole rather than reviews of component functions (for example, configuration management). Other modules in the IT Infrastructure Library provide guidance on how to establish specific service management functions.

This module is primarily concerned with organizational structure, roles and responsibilities. It does not address in detail the staffing requirements for individual functions at the operational level. The module covers the issues of organizational culture and management of change in broad terms, and refers to other relevant CCTA guidance where this is possible.

2.4 Related guidance

This module is one of a series that constitute the CCTA IT Infrastructure Library. Although the module is structured in such a way that it can be read in isolation, it is recommended that it is used in conjunction with other modules.

All IT Infrastructure Library modules have some relevance to the organizational structure of IT Services. Of particular relevance are other modules in the Managers' Set:

* Planning and Control for IT Services

* Quality Management for IT Services

* Customer Liaison

* Managing Supplier Relationships

* Managing Facilities Management.

CCTA also produces a range of guidance relevant to organizations which are considering or undertaking market testing of IS/IT services. The Market Testing IS/IT booklet **The In-house Bid** is particularly relevant to internal IT organizations bidding to provide future services after market testing.

2.5 Standards

ISO9001/EN29001/BS5750 Part 1 - Quality Management and Quality Assurance Standards

The IT Infrastructure Library modules are designed to assist adherents, for example organizations' IT Directorates, to obtain third-party quality certification to ISO9001. Such third parties should be accredited by the NACCB, the National Accreditation Council for Certification Bodies.

ISEB Certificate in Service Management

The Information Systems Examination Board (ISEB) administers a proficiency-certification scheme for IT service management practitioners, including trainers and consultants. CCTA recommends that contractors and consultants, as well as internal staff, employed by Government Departments to assist with management of IT service provision are qualified, wherever possible, by possession of the ISEB Certificate in Service Management - or an equivalent.

(CCTA's IS Notice 29, October 1991 refers).

3. Planning the IT Services Organization

3.0 Context

Sections 3, 4 and 5 of this module provide a framework for an organizational review, and for planning and implementing changes to the organizational structure of the IT Services Organization. The following sections (3.0.1 to 3.0.4) place the IT Services Organization in the wider context and introduce some concepts relevant to organizational design.

3.0.1 IS provision

Traditionally, information systems (IS) services have been provided from the centre of organizations as a common service to other areas. In recent years, however, there has been a clear trend towards devolving responsibility for IS to business areas - a trend paralleled in other areas such as finance and personnel. Three distinct types of IS provision can be identified - centralized, fully decentralized, and a mixed or federal model where responsibility is shared. These are outlined below.

More generally, parent organizations can themselves be seen to be unitary or federal entities. In the latter case, there would be a number of discrete business areas existing within an overall management framework. The creation of Next Steps Agencies has been an important factor in increasing the number of organizations of this type.

There is considerable research evidence that the arrangements for IS provision should match the form of the parent organization. That is, unitary parent organizations are likely to be best served by centralized IS provision, while federal parent organizations will call for decentralized or federal IS provision.

Centralized/common service provision

Where IT provision is centralized, the IT Directorate is responsible for all IT services and resources (see figure 1). Although equipment may be distributed around customer locations it is centrally coordinated, controlled and managed. The advantages of this approach include:

* economies of scale from organization-wide infrastructure and sharing of resources

* bringing together scarce IT skills and providing a career structure within the IT Directorate

**Figure 1:
Centralized
IT Provision**

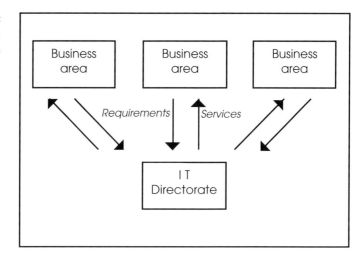

* minimizing infrastructure management overheads by centralizing responsibility for contingency and capacity planning etc

* scope for formalizing service delivery with Service Level Agreements (SLAs), charging policy etc.

Disadvantages in this approach include:

* business areas do not control day-to-day provision of IS services

* prioritization may be outside the control of the business unit

* corporate policies may constrain the options available to the business units.

Decentralized/distributed IS resources

Advantages of decentralizing responsibility for service provision to business units include:

* prioritization of the activities of the IS providers is in the hands of the business unit's management and conflicts of interest are reduced

* the IS providers are close to the business, can align themselves with its objectives and are responsive to changing business requirements.

Disadvantages of a decentralized approach include:

* it is difficult to achieve economies of scale and there may be a tendency for business units to 'reinvent the wheel'

* developing systems which meet the needs of each business unit in isolation may prevent future integration of information or restructuring of business boundaries.

In a fully decentralized situation, IT services are provided by the business areas themselves with no central IT services provider.

Since this module focuses on the role of the IT Directorate as a central provider of services, service management in a fully decentralized scenario is outside its scope. Nevertheless, the module does point to issues which must be faced by business areas in the fully decentralized scenario. Similar issues will apply whatever the size of organization, although the number of people with direct responsibility for service management may be small.

Federal model

Many organizations adopt a combination of centralized and decentralized models (see figure 2). In this case, service provision responsibilities are split between the IT Directorate - which may provide shared infrastructure and common services - and business areas (each of which may have its own IT unit). In this situation, clear divisions of responsibility are particularly important. The IT Directorate may adopt a wide range of management styles reflecting the degree of influence it has (for example whether it directs, coordinates or gives guidance) over decisions the business units take about IT.

**Figure 2:
Federal IT
Provision**

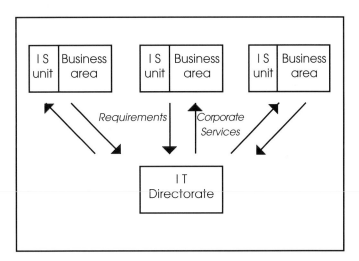

The degree to which responsibility and authority for IT is centralized or devolved to business areas is an important organizational issue and will affect:

* the balance of IT resource and budget between the IT Directorate and business areas

* the boundary of management responsibility for activities such as procurement

* the structure of, and parties to, Service Level Agreements

* the structure required for effective customer liaison such as the use of centralized or decentralized Help Desks

* the potential for adequate contingency arrangements.

The **Management of Local Processors and Terminals** module gives guidance about managing IT resources (such as personal computers, local area network servers, minicomputers) which are distributed among business areas. It emphasizes the need to coordinate service management activities when responsibilities for IT are divided between the IT Directorate and business areas.

3.0.2 Market testing

The Competing for Quality initiative and the associated *market testing* programmes of Central Government are leading many Departments to test their internal IS service provision against alternative sources of supply in order to ensure value for money. Similar initiatives exist in Local Government, while many private sector organizations are also considering the scope for contracting out some or all their IT services to a third party.

Even without market testing, many organizations will consider using external providers of IT services. The IT Services Organization may, for example, subcontract some services such as hardware maintenance which underpin the SLAs it has with its customers.

Although market testing does not imply that contracting out will be the chosen route, services chosen for market testing must be capable of provision through external suppliers.

One impact of market testing IS/IT services is that the IT Directorate, or part of it, may have to compete against external providers to provide a service. Section 3.1.5.3

describes some of the potential impacts a move towards working on a more commercial footing may have on the IT Services Organization.

The *Intelligent Customer*   Market testing requires a clearer separation of the roles of customer and provider, and places new demands on customers. Tasks that had previously been the province of the IT Directorate may become the customer's responsibility.

In this situation the onus is firmly upon managers in business areas to ensure that their requirements for IT services, which support business objectives, are met. Customers need to acquire *intelligent customer* capabilities - the ability to plan, specify, acquire, implement and use IS to achieve business objectives.

The *intelligent customer* function embodies the role of the Service Control Team (see below) and will be responsible for service control whether or not an in-house or external IT provider is used.

There is no single recommended approach to organizing the intelligent customer function. The options cover a wide spectrum. For example, business areas may set up their own intelligent customer functions; or the existing IT Directorate may set up an intelligent customer function to serve its existing customer base.

More information on roles and responsibilities for service control in the market testing context is provided in the CCTA booklet **The *Intelligent Customer***.

Service Control Team   The IT Infrastructure Library module, **Managing Facilities Management**, points to the need to be able to control relationships with external providers and describes the role of a service control team (SCT).

The SCT is responsible for:

*   carrying out the planning activities for, and overseeing the implementation of contracted services

*   overseeing the ongoing management of contracts

*   monitoring quality measures

*   quality auditing of each provider's processes

*   acting as the main interface to providers on all service-related matters

*   overseeing any handover at the end of contracts

13

* generally looking after the customers' interests and overseeing the smooth running of SLAs on their behalf.

The Managing Facilities Management module describes a situation in which the IT Services Organization acts on behalf of the parent organization but the same principles apply for a business customer managing an in-house provider after market testing, or where the IT Services Organization has subcontracted some services.

3.0.3 The IT Directorate

The IT Directorate acts as the in-house provider of IT services to the parent organization. Organizational structure varies but as a general model, the IT Directorate consists of a number of groups, including one or more responsible for the IT Directorate's main business services such as software development, software maintenance and the delivery of operational IT services (see figure 3).

**Figure 3:
The IT
Directorate**

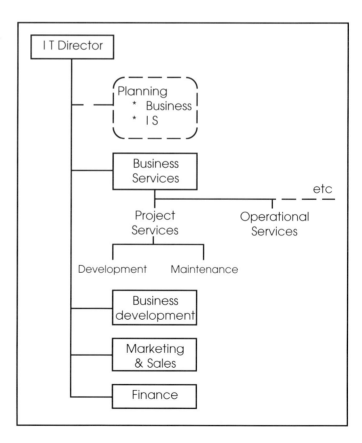

Other administrative groups, such as finance and human resource development (or personnel), may exist, and there may be separate groups for corporate issues such as quality management, security, or planning. A marketing and sales function is increasingly common where relationships between IT Directorates and their customers are becoming more formal.

The heads of each group, along with the IT Director, are likely to constitute the IT Directorate's Management Team.

Organizations should develop corporate policies covering issues such as quality, security, finance, contingency or personnel which will apply throughout the organization.

3.0.4 The IT Services Organization

In general the IT Services Organization, as provider of operational IT services, will be a discrete part of the IT Directorate. This reflects the different skills required and the nature of services it provides compared to, say, applications development and maintenance. It must be emphasized however that organizing IT Services cannot be considered in isolation from the rest of the IT Directorate and indeed of the wider parent organization.

The successful provision of operational IT services requires a systematic approach to service management. The purpose of service management is to ensure:

* the delivery of services which meet customers requirements

* that services can be measured and compared with stated target service levels

* that disruption to services is minimized and can be managed

* that costs related to the delivery of services are clearly and completely identified and are justified.

Figure 4, overleaf, indicates a logical model of service management functions, although boundaries are not rigid. (For example most functions will have a planning element, not simply those under service planning and monitoring.) It is not intended as a recommended organizational structure although some of the groupings shown will often be exhibited in organizational structures, particularly in Customer Services and Operations units.

Figure 4:
Model of
Service
Management

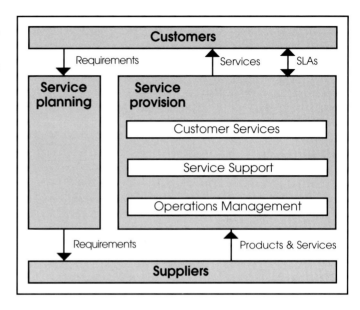

Service planning

Service management functions which contribute to the planning of operational IT services include:

* service level management

* cost management

* availability management

* capacity management

* contingency planning.

Each of these functions also embodies a monitoring element to ensure that, for example, service availability levels which have been planned and included in Service Level Agreements are actually met in practice.

Customers must be fully involved in planning and designing services. During market testing, it is important to note that the services that will be required may not be the same as those which are provided currently. The IT Services Organization may need to be changed to deliver these new services.

Planning the delivery of operational IT services must be carried out in the context of the IT Directorate's planning framework and in accord with longer term infrastructure plans, and technical policies. Further information on this can be found in the **Planning and Control for IT Services** module.

Customer services

Once the service requirements have been agreed, the relationship between the customers and the IT Services Organization is via the customer services function. This will have a fundamental impact on the way services are perceived by customers. Customer services functions include:

* Help Desk

* customer liaison activities (such as account management and marketing).

The interface between the IT Services Organization and customers is considered in section 3.1.5.2.

Service support

Service support is concerned with the effective management of services, with coordinating, monitoring and controlling the resources which deliver services. This includes control over changes required during the implementation as well as day-to-day running of the IT infrastructure. Relevant functions are:

* problem management

* change management

* configuration management

* software control and distribution.

These functions are concerned less with managing specific elements of the IT infrastructure than with information about the service overall (such as incidents or problems, and changes required to the service). In contrast, operations management is concerned with specific elements (or domains) of the IT Infrastructure.

Operations management

A number of functions are directly concerned with planning, managing and operating the technical resources which make up the IT infrastructure:

* computer operations management

* network services management

* management of local processors and terminals.

Operations management may encompass technical support of the infrastructure, whether it is provided by internal or external sources (hardware technical support for example, is particularly likely to be provided by a hardware supplier).

Installation of equipment also needs to be controlled and in some cases, such as procurement and installation of large computers, may need to be run as a project (see the **Computer Installation and Acceptance** module).

Aspects of the environment within which IT infrastructure is situated and used - buildings, offices, computer centres, cables, power, noise, lighting etc - must also be managed.

Coordination and liaison

As well as liaison with customers, there is a need for coordination, communication and liaison with various other interests outside the IT Services Organization. These include:

* liaison with people responsible for developing and maintaining applications software whether within, or external to, the IT Directorate to ensure service management interests are addressed (see the **Software Lifecycle Support** module) and in particular in testing (see the **Testing an IT Service for Operational Use** module)

* management of relationships with suppliers of products and services to the IT Services Organization and its customers, for example suppliers of hardware, software, third party maintenance etc (see **Managing Supplier Relationships, Managing Facilities Management, Third Party and Single Source Maintenance** modules)

* coordination of, or liaison with others responsible for, corporate issues including quality, security, contingency, finance and personnel; and coordination of planning and control activities. (This may result in an element of matrix management whereby staff in the IT Services Organization with, for example, security responsibilities, will need to report to both line and functional management.)

Annex B provides a brief description of service management functions covered by the IT Infrastructure Library.

Annex D includes example role descriptions.

3.1 Procedures

Ongoing monitoring of the business environment and the performance of the IT Services Organization (see figure 4) will identify numerous small changes and adaptations which need to be made within the existing organizational structure. A more radical review of the organization is sometimes required, especially when the IT Directorate faces the prospect of major changes triggered by, for example:

* changes in the business environment (for example market testing, privatization, a significant shift in business strategy)

* a drive to new, more formal, relationships between customers and provider (perhaps signalled by the introduction of Service Level Agreements or charges for services)

* a drive towards improved value for money from IT resources (including moves towards market testing and contracting out)

* a drive towards quality improvement (part of ISO9001)

* a new requirement to compete directly with alternative providers

* a major shift in the hardware and software platforms on which services will be delivered

* a radical change in the required services (eg introduction of terminals on a one-per-desk basis, office automation, introduction of a major new service or application)

* serious problems meeting, or a steady decline in ability to meet, Service Level Agreements

* worsening customer perceptions of the services delivered.

In principle any project charged with carrying out a review or with planning change needs to consider three key questions:

* where are we now?

* where do we want to be?

* how do we get there?

In an organizational review of IT Services, understanding "where we are now" involves gaining an understanding of the current organization, the business environment in which it operates, and its performance.

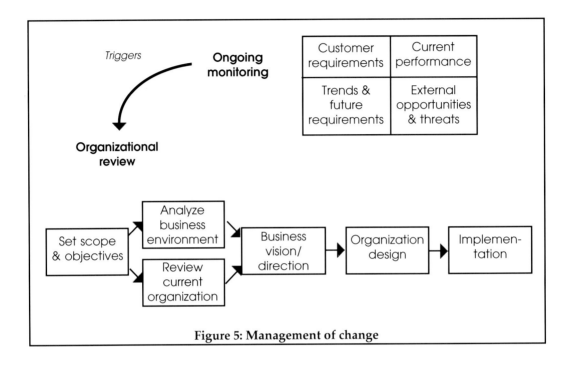

Figure 5: Management of change

Deciding where the IT Services Organization wants to be, in organizational terms, involves deciding what the organization structure should be and how it should operate given its business environment, expectations about future requirements, and its place within the IT Directorate and parent organization.

Getting to where IT Services wants to be involves determining a change programme which will move the organization from its present to its required position.

Carrying out an organizational review and implementing organizational changes may be managed as a project, or as a programme of inter-related projects. Reviews and changes of the IT Services Organization will often be part of a wider programme of review and change. For example, there may be associated projects to enact change to other parts of the organization, to change business practices or introduce IT systems. Guidance on project management is available in the PRINCE method.

The approach described in this module is not intended to be prescriptive. It indicates issues and activities to be considered in the context of any programme or project management method which is adopted.

Initiation of an organizational review and approval of any proposed changes which result from it will rest with the IT Services Manager, the IT Director or with other senior management groups such as the IS Steering Committee or IT Executive Committee. Customer involvement in the Project Board may serve to ensure that any changes introduced meet customers requirements.

The IT Services Manager must take overall responsibility for reviews and changes specifically concerned with the IT Services Organization.

For major projects an organizational review team will be required and members may need to work on the project on a full time basis.

3.1.1 Set scope and objectives for organizational review

Establishing project scope and objectives is an important step since it will condition to a large extent the way the review is conducted. If the review is a response to a pressing problem there may be little time for detailed analysis or for a formal project. Nevertheless, time spent analysing the problem at the outset will be repaid by the increased likelihood of identifying the most appropriate solution.

In order to help define both the scope and objectives, the following should be identified:

* the project sponsor

* why the review is taking place

* aims of the review

* deliverables

* parts of the IT Directorate which will be looked at

* parts of the IT Directorate which will be excluded

* priorities

* risks

* who will carry out the review

* how the review will be carried out (interviews, questionnaires etc)

* measures to help check that objectives have been achieved, if possible

* overall timescales

* management and reporting arrangements.

The project objectives should be set out in a project initiation document. Detailed objectives for the project may be handed to the review team at the outset, or there may be an expectation that broad objectives will be refined and clarified. In many cases objectives will be soft (concerned with cultural change as well as organizational structure perhaps) or difficult to measure (improving communication for example). In other cases objectives may be explicit (such as a requirement to design a structure of no more than a given number of management layers).

Inputs to the review may include business strategies and IS strategy reports (at corporate and business area level, and for the IT Directorate), other organizational reviews and audits, quality reviews, problem reports, customer liaison reports etc.

3.1.2 Analysis of business environment

An organizational review must include, or take account of an existing, analysis of the current business environment. This should attempt to identify trends and probable changes in the business environment, in particular those which will place new or different demands and requirements upon the IT Services Organization, and customers' requirements. (The review may be able to draw on existing strategy study reports for this information.)

This analysis should influence the future strategy of the IT Services Organization, not just its structure.

A review of the business environment is required which asks questions such as:

* what are our customers' requirements?

* what changes are taking place in our customers' business environment?

* what changes that affect the IT Services Organization can be anticipated?

* what trends can be seen?

* what strategies are other organizations (such as other suppliers of IS services) pursuing?

* what new demands and constraints will be placed on the IT Services Organization?

Figure 6 illustrates some of the elements of an IT Services Organization's business environment.

The precise composition of the business environment will of course depend upon the particular situation of each IT Services Organization.

Figure 6 shows the immediate business environment of the IT Services Organization to include the parent organization as a whole and separate business areas, suppliers, competitors and partners (eg where a business alliance with an external organization depends on interworking IT systems). If the IT Services Organization has a high degree of autonomy, other parts of the IT Directorate may need to be considered as separate elements.

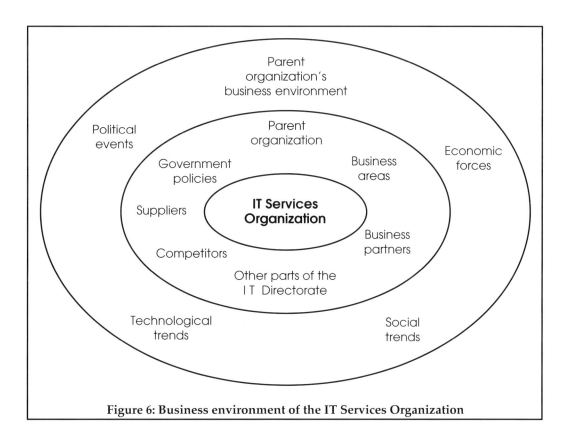

Figure 6: Business environment of the IT Services Organization

Organizational trends in the parent organization are likely to be reflected in the IT Services Organization. For example, current trends and drivers include cost containment or reduction, market testing, greater responsibility for IT being shifted to business areas and moves towards flatter organizations with fewer layers of management, and shorter information and decision-making chains.

Beyond these immediate elements lies the wider business environment within which the parent organization operates and a broad range of social, political, economic and technological trends and forces which constrain and influence the operation of all organizations.

The results of a review of the business environment can be expressed as a set of planning assumptions; in effect a best guess at what the future holds. Alternatively, if divergent futures can be identified, the output may be a set of scenarios - different possible futures. Since the business environment is not static, planning assumptions must be kept under review.

3.1.3 Review of current organization

The existing IT Services Organization should be reviewed to provide a baseline for assessing the success of any organizational changes which are introduced. A review of the current IT Services Organization should consider:

* aims and objectives of the IT Services Organization (including any available mission or goal statements)

* the IT Services Organization's position within, and relations with, other parts of the IT Directorate

* how effectively the IT Services Organization is seen to support the business (in terms of meeting Service Level Agreements and in terms of customer perceptions)

* costs and whether the current IT Services Organization is seen to provide value for money

* whether there are duplicated, overlapping or conflicting activities

* the need for new, or changes in the role of, service management functions

* activities not required in future (such as support of obsolete systems)

* reasons for current structure

* current staffing levels (numbers, grades and skills)

* strengths and weaknesses perceived by management, staff and customers.

Carrying out such a review must aim to clarify and make explicit the objectives of IT Services, if they are not already clear.

A concise definition of purpose for the IT Services Organization, possibly expressed as a mission statement, should be produced if one is not already available. This will support the mission of the IT Directorate and that of the parent organization. The structure of the IT Services Organization should be reviewed in the light of how it supports the mission statement. Likewise the objectives of the project should aim to ensure IT Services can comply with its mission statement.

The strengths and weaknesses of the existing organization should be considered both from an internal viewpoint and from that of other stakeholders. Getting the opinion of customers is particularly valuable. Customers may have views on the efficiency and effectiveness of IT Services as a whole or of particular functions, and of the adequacy of staffing levels. Similarly staff in IT Services will have views about the existing organizational structure and working practices. Appropriate techniques, including questionnaires and interviews, can help capture information about perceptions of IT Services.

3.1.4 Future direction and strategy

In the light of the analysis of the present state and future business environment, it will be possible to make explicit the future direction and strategy of the IT Services Organization. This is likely to be concerned with:

* the extent to which services are to be provided centrally or decentralized

* which services will be offered by the IT Services Organization

* how it will respond to issues such as market testing

* its response to trends such as open systems and downsizing.

Decisions on these issues will need to be taken by the IT Services Organization management team, or more probably by that of the IT Directorate as a whole, but the project team can make proposals or provide information to aid the decision making process. Once these decisions have been made, a solid foundation will be available upon which to design the future organization.

3.1.5 Organizational design

Organizational design includes:

* the definition of processes which support delivery of the required services and the proper flow of information

* designing the organizational structure and defining roles and responsibilities

* identifying the need for skills

* identifying the need for links across and outside the organization, including contact with customers and suppliers

* job design.

Customer requirements along with other aspects of the business environment are the basis for deciding what services will be provided. Decisions about service processes and functions, skills and organizational culture, and the organizational structure of the IT Services Organization derive from customer requirements and the type of service that will be provided. There can therefore be no single, ideal organizational design to suit all IT Services organizations.

The review team will be able to identify a number of options for how IT Services could be structured and will need to assess the degree to which each option will meet the stated objectives.

Organizational design must address how the planned organization will operate. This involves:

* identifying and designing the processes which link functions together, including processes which extend beyond the IT Services Organization

* addressing the cultural norms and values which guide people's behaviour

* the need to supplement the organizational structure by decision-making committees and teams brought together for particular purposes

* facilitating cross-functional teams and communication to ensure people do not develop a narrow focus on functional responsibilities at the expense of meeting the overall business need.

The IT Infrastructure Library provides guidance on a range of service management functions (where a function is a logical set of tasks and activities such as Change Management) which underpin effective service processes. A number of management roles (such as the Change Manager) are also identified. Roles do not necessarily equate to jobs, people or grades. A role may be carried out by several people, or may be combined with other roles and carried out by one person. Example role descriptions included in Annex D may be used as the basis for defining specific job descriptions.

3.1.5.1 Distinguish between front and back office activities

A distinction can be made between (back-office) functions whose prime role is to manage the production of services; and (front-office) functions which involve a direct interaction with customers.

Distinguishing between front and back office functions provides a possible basis for a broad grouping of functions in the organizational structure. The distinction is better understood as a spectrum, one view of which is illustrated in figure 7 (overleaf), rather than a rigid division.

Front office, or customer-oriented, functions (such as Service Level Management, Customer Liaison and Help Desk) may be grouped in order to:

* improve coordination and communications

* bring together functions with related skills and information requirements

* simplify communication channels for customers - for example by establishing a single Help Desk to deal with all calls from users.

Front-office functions require good interpersonal skills. Back-office functions tend to depend more on technical abilities, which have traditionally been emphasized in IT

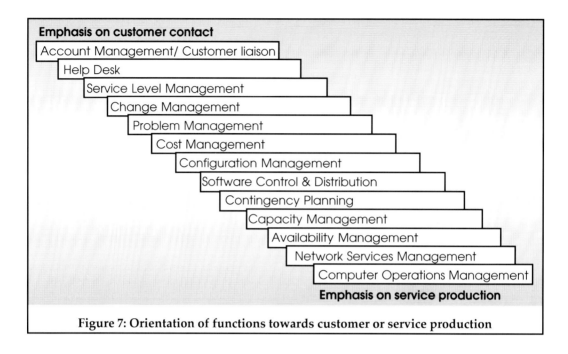

Figure 7: Orientation of functions towards customer or service production

Directorates. Raising the profile of customer-oriented functions indicates to both IT staff and customers the importance to the IT Services Organization of developing good relationships as well as meeting target service levels.

Recognizing a broad distinction between front and back office functions, and the need for different skills, should not obscure the need for processes linking customer and production-oriented staff. For example, the Help Desk has often been placed within the operations group because it is closely linked with day-to-day delivery and support of services. The need for good communications between the Help Desk and computer operations and network control staff may be met by their co-location in an Operations Bridge (see the **Computer Operations Management** module) even if they are in separate line management commands.

Management and operation of the various elements of the IT infrastructure (computers, networks, software) requires specialist skills. As a result, distinct organizational groups have tended to emerge, eg for network management and computer operations management. The need to coordinate control of the IT infrastructure supports the move towards grouping, or at least improving the coordination, of these functions.

3.1.5.2 The customer interface

Organizational design for service delivery organizations must seek to ensure:

* that customers have easy access to and simple channels of communication with the service provider

* that the customer is supported as "a whole person" ie the customer should as far as possible have a single point of contact with the service provider

* that staff understand the importance of supporting, and developing good relationships with, customers.

Organizational design approaches which can meet these requirements include:

* making it easy for the customer to contact the IT Services Organization by, for example, having one help desk to deal with all types of systems incident and enquiry

* basing the entire organizational structure of the IT Services Organization around client groups.

The latter approach, in which the service provider is divided into groups dedicated to particular clients, is usually introduced to improve customer service because the structure is focused on supporting clearly identified customers. (This is similar to creating product centred groups in manufacturing organizations each of which has its own marketing, production and sales resource.) If all the service provider's staff are placed in such client centred groups, there will be, in effect, a duplicated functional structure (as each client group will have its own support functions, operations groups etc). This approach may be appropriate for discrete services delivered to clearly separate groups of customers.

In practice, most IT Directorates do not support customers, services and infrastructures which are so independent that they require entirely separate service provider structures to support them.

Therefore most IT Directorates will require a combination of client-oriented staff (such as account managers dedicated to particular customers) and functional groups for infrastructure management and operations making the most efficient use of specialist skills and resources.

Nature of contact

Differences in the nature of contacts between IT Services and customers, the people involved and their concerns need to be understood. The IT Infrastructure Library **Customer Liaison** module describes various contacts between IT Services and its customers. The majority of contacts with customers will be handled by:

* the Help Desk, which has the main day-to-day contact, dealing with incidents and requests for help, and disseminating information

* Account Managers and/or the Service Level Manager, who will manage the overall quality of IT service provision and oversee Service Level Agreements

* the IT Director and the IT Services Manager, who are involved in agreeing IT policies, strategies with customers and future service plans.

On the customer side, there may be scope to channel communication through a customer coordinator (described in the **Customer Liaison** module) or, if equipment is distributed through business areas, by introducing Local Systems Administrators (discussed in the **Management of Local Processors and Terminals** module; a role description is provided in Annex D).

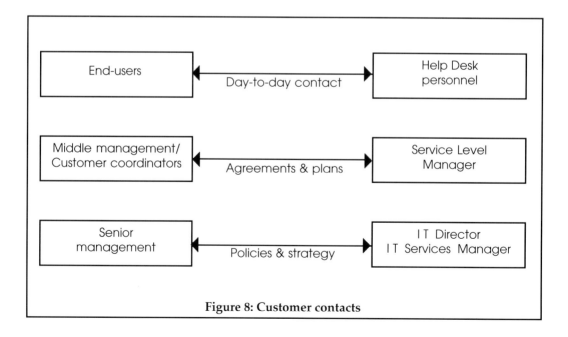

Figure 8: Customer contacts

3.1.5.3 Operating as a separate business unit

Increasingly the clear separation of roles of IT provider and customer, even within the same parent organization, is leading to the need for the IT Directorate to operate in a more commercial way. In some cases the IT Directorate will charge for services, either to recover costs or to make a profit. Initiatives such as *market testing* or compulsory competitive tendering mean that the in-house provider of IT services must increasingly be able to compete with external providers of services.

The need to compete will place even greater emphasis on the need to minimize the costs of delivering services and will have a number of organizational impacts.

As the marketing and selling of services takes on a higher priority, certain activities will gain prominence:

* account management

* marketing

* sales

* business development.

These are closely linked activities. The way they are carried out will depend on factors such as whether the IT Directorate may provide services to customers outside the parent organization and whether it must make a profit.

Account management

Faced with the need to improve the interface with customers and to obtain information about future requirements, some organizations establish an account management function which can provide a common interface to the customer for all of the IT Directorate's business services. Account Managers will usually be concerned to identify business requirements and strategy and to translate these into requirements for IT services, and in some cases will take on much of the Service Level Manager role.

Account management can also be seen as an extension of the role of Customer Liaison Manager (see Annex D). Each Account Manager is typically given responsibility for the relationship with a customer or group of customers. The Customer Liaison module considers a range of liaison and support activities which would form the basis for an account management function.

Account management usually involves a degree of marketing which is likely to increase if the IT Directorate must compete with external providers.

Marketing and sales

Market testing and the loss of the automatic right to provide services is a major change for an in-house provider. More effort is required to establish customers' requirements, to persuade customers of the benefits of using the in-house provider and to win the right to provide services. Marketing and sales functions gain prominence in these circumstances.

While marketing and sales are closely related they can be distinguished as follows:

* marketing is concerned with understanding potential customer needs, ensuring the needs are satisfied by the services offered and influencing the adaptation of services as customers needs evolve

* sales involves meeting a specific customers need competitively, for example through a market test.

Marketing is a continuous activity of which promoting the IT Directorate's services and capabilities is only part. It includes:

* identifying and influencing customers requirements

* ensuring customers are informed about all services provided by the IT Directorate including, particularly during market testing, those which may be hidden or easily overlooked (such as informal advice)

* promoting a professional image for the IT Directorate and its services

* gathering information from customers about their needs for, and perceptions of, services.

Internal customers will often be concerned about the impact that marketing and related activities, as cost overheads, will have on the cost of the services they use. Introducing marketing groups and practices requires great care. Large numbers of glossy brochures are not necessary and may cause an adverse reaction.

Bidding for business during market testing exercises is likely to require a team with responsibility for developing bids. The responsibilities of the team which develops in-house bids are distinct from those of the management of the in-house provider and the bidding team is likely to exist for the duration of the bidding exercise rather than being a permanent part of the organizational structure. Further guidance is provided in the CCTA Market Testing IS/IT booklet, The In-house Bid.

Business development

The IT Directorate needs to be able to develop new products and services required by customers, and may need to carry out research and development to this end.

If the IT Directorate operates on a profit-making basis, it will need to make decisions about the commercial viability of services. This signals the need to have relevant commercial, financial and legal skills, and for sound business planning.

3.1.5.4 Constraints on organizational design

Designing the structure of the IT Services Organization must address a wide range of factors which may act as constraints on the organizational design options. A review of the IT Services Organization may be able to challenge aspects of the current organization. For example the review may be able to suggest reducing the number of mainframe operations sites. If this is not acceptable, organizational design must work within the constraints given. The nature of constraints will vary greatly; possible issues include:

* location of customers

    - is there a need for local Help Desks, Local Systems Administrators, or technical support staff to support a dispersed customer population?

    - is there a risk that the IT Services Organization will be perceived as remote from customers on distant sites?

* location of IT staff

    - are there communication and coordination difficulties between staff in different locations?

    - which functions can and should be centralized?

    - which functions should be dispersed over several locations (eg using Local Systems Administration for customer support)?

* size of the IT Services Organization

    - can all service management functions be
      adequately supported, and are they all relevant to
      the services provided?

    - in large organizations there is more scope for
      separating functional specialisms, but usually
      more risk of coordination and communication
      difficulties

    - for smaller organizations, communication
      problems may be reduced, but developing
      sufficient in-house specialist skills may be
      difficult.

* nature of the IT infrastructure

    - does the organization support a single or a multi-
      vendor architecture? What is the requirement for
      specialist skills to support different hardware and
      software?

    - can service management functions and roles be
      categorized as either dependent on a single
      platform or common to a number of platforms,
      and staffed accordingly?

* the use, or availability, of software tools to support
  service management functions

    - can the use of service management support tools
      enable efficiency savings by supporting common
      data needs or improving information flows?

Organizations operating a complex IT infrastructure which
includes hardware and software platforms of different
types, or from many suppliers, may be inclined to use these
differences as the principal basis on which to structure the
IT Services Organization.

While this approach may reflect a genuine need for
specialist skills, it can lead to duplication of functions and
roles. Platform-based groups are most likely to be
appropriate if each platform supports a distinct group of
customers with little need for integration. Increasingly
differences in technology must be made transparent to users
and single organizational interfaces to service management
functions including Help Desk, service level management
and change management are required, irrespective of the
hardware and software platforms on which services are
delivered.

3.1.6 Job design

Having defined a proposed organizational structure based on a logical view of what is required, it is necessary to identify people to fill posts. This involves identifying:

* proposed roles and required skills

* existing staff, skills and experience

* shortfalls in existing skills

* ways of addressing shortfall (training, recruitment, consultancy).

Collecting this information will be easier if there are existing records of staff skills, and experience and training logs. Maintaining such information, perhaps by means of a central skills register, may be the responsibility of the IT Directorate's (or the parent organization's) Personnel section. If such information is not currently available, the process of assigning staff may offer an opportunity to build up a skills register.

It is essential that functions and roles are considered from the position of need and the value they add to the delivered IT services. Organizations must ask which activities are necessary; and which are desirable but could be left out, or reduced in scope.

For smaller organizations it is particularly important to consider the functions and roles described in this module as logical elements, rather than assuming that a separate person is required to carry out each role. If the need for a function is not great, a role may amount to only a small part of someone's job.

The important thing is to carry out each function to a level appropriate for the needs of the organization.

The **Human Factors in the Office Environment** module identifies the following basic principles of good job design:

* combination of tasks to form a coherent whole job, the performance of which makes a significant contribution to the IT Directorate's objectives which is recognizable by the job holder

* performance indicators should be known to staff so that they can recognize improvements and shortfalls

* provision of some variety of pace, method, location and skill

* inclusion of some degree of responsibility for the end product.

Differences in responsibility must be clear. For example, who has overall management responsibility for a function; who collects and analyzes information; who needs access to information etc?

Comparing proposed with existing job descriptions may identify tasks which have been omitted in the proposed structure (any omissions in the implemented structure should be by design not accident!) and bring to light any misunderstandings about whether and how functions have been carried out in the past and what is required in the future.

Regrouping responsibilities offers an opportunity to eliminate any duplication of effort that has grown up in the existing organization. There may be opportunities to automate tasks cost effectively (for example by introducing automated or unattended operating). Automation can enable the redeployment of staff to alternative, and perhaps priority tasks providing they have or can be trained to acquire the required skills.

3.1.6.1   Staff numbers

Organizations vary too much for any guidance to be given with confidence on how many staff will be required in IT Services. Numbers will depend on particular circumstances.

For an existing IT Services Organization the number of staff required can often be judged by breaking down current work, identifying the time taken to carry out tasks and how functions will be grouped in any revised structure. By assessing the workload of each post it should be possible to assess how many staff (more or less than current) are required. Grading will depend on levels of responsibility and the importance of each function.

New organizations do not have existing practices against which to map future needs. Identifying organizations doing similar work and visiting them to compare tasks and see if meaningful comparisons can be made is a useful approach.

Some companies offer commercial services which compare costs and staff numbers (amongst other criteria) of one organization with those of other comparable organizations. This offers a baseline for assessing internal organizational structures and costs.

Comparing existing staff numbers and skills with the proposed structure will identify any shortages or surpluses. The number of staff required must take into account the need to cover for absences, potential staff turnover, career paths and succession planning, and the need for staff at managerial and operational/support levels. Liaison with personnel departments will ensure any corporate staffing policies are identified. If the new structure will require fewer people, options for redeployment or redundancy must be identified and communicated to staff.

In planning the assignment of staff the capabilities of specific managers must be taken into account. The number of staff any manager will be expected to manage should be considered (there may be corporate guidance on maximum span of command) as should grades (Job Evaluation and Grading section of HM Treasury publish guidance on grading for IT posts in the Civil Service).

3.1.6.2 Role descriptions

Annex D provides a number of role descriptions which may be used as a basis for defining job descriptions. This may involve combining a number of roles into one job or separating elements of roles into several jobs. For example, the roles of Configuration Manager, Change Manager and Problem Manager may in some instances be carried out by one person.

Market testing and other pressures to ensure value for money, reduce costs and constrain staff numbers emphasize the need to carry out only those tasks which are necessary, and to combine roles where this is feasible.

Matching staff against the logical structure may lead to some modifications in the proposed organization, perhaps because of short term skills shortages. The design process should, however, have identified requirements for training or recruitment to resolve such shortages in the longer term.

3.1.7 The implementation plan

Deciding whether the proposed IT Services Organization can be implemented in one pass or if a phased approach is required will depend on the scale of the change and the resources (people and budgets) available to carry out the project, and the urgency of the change. The need to manage existing services whilst restructuring may also constrain the way implementation is carried out.

The introduction of service management functions or changes in the way functions are carried out cannot be considered in isolation. Such changes will usually have an effect on the IT Directorate as a whole.

The implementation plan should identify:

* functions which are to be introduced, regrouped or redefined

* priorities for introducing, changing or reducing functions

* any changes required outside the IT Services Organization

* clear responsibilities for implementing all changes

* timescales with key milestones

* measures to assess achievement and improvement

* communications and awareness initiatives

* recruitment and training

* requirements for service management support tools

* accommodation/environmental requirements

* any requirements for short term staff, contractors or consultants.

Responsibility for planning the introduction of new, or for changing existing, functions will usually rest with designated function managers. Other modules in the IT Infrastructure Library provide guidance on the implementation of specific service management functions.

Introducing functions

The order in which service management functions will be introduced depends on objectives and priorities. If, for example, IT Services is seeking to become more customer oriented, the customer interface may be the prime issue; while the need to reduce costs or introduce charging for IT services may make cost management the priority.

The IT Services Organization must be able to carry out the necessary planning and control activities to ensure it can meet SLAs. This rests on the introduction of appropriate service management processes. The interdependence of service management functions means it is difficult to introduce service management as a series of isolated functions.

Introducing SLAs without the underlying means of planning, monitoring and rectifying problems with services leads to a high risk of introducing SLAs which cannot be met.

Nevertheless, there may be pressure to introduce SLAs quickly. A compromise might be to produce draft SLAs at the same time as establishing underpinning service management functions, renegotiating SLAs on a firmer basis later.

Failure to ensure meaningful, achievable, SLAs at the first attempt can damage the credibility of the IT Services Organization; credibility which it may be difficult to recover. Therefore if draft or provisional SLAs are to be introduced, their status must be clear and agreed with customers at the outset, with a timescale for establishing revised agreements.

Detailed information about dependencies between specific functions is given in other modules in the IT Infrastructure Library.

The CCTA IS Planning Subject Guide, **Prioritization**, includes guidance on establishing the relative importance of information systems. Many of the techniques described therein could be used in assessing priorities for organizational change.

3.2 Dependencies

The organizational review and the planning of changes to the IT Services Organization depends on many factors, including:

* clearly defined purpose and objectives

* commitment to the review and change projects from senior managers including the IT Director and IT Services Manager

* a clear understanding of customers and their requirements

* having enough people with the right skills to carry out the review and to produce change plans

* the co-operation of people outside the IT Services Organization who will be affected by change (including customers and staff in other parts of the IT Directorate)

* knowledge of any constraints on planning options.

3.3 People

3.3.1 IT Services Manager

The IT Services Manager has overall responsibility for the IT Services Organization and must sponsor any organizational review or change programme. A role description for the IT Services Manager is included at Annex D.

If a project to review or implement changes to IT Services is required, day-to-day responsibility may be delegated to an organizational review team.

3.3.2 Organization review team/change team

The larger the organization the more likely that a team will be required to carry out the organizational review and plan any resulting change programme. People involved in the review and in carrying through the change programme may or may not be the same people; but it must be recognized that these are distinct stages.

If the project is likely to be lengthy, ideally the team members will be removed from their current responsibilities. Using external staff to help review, design, plan and implement changes to the organization may also bring an independent view and wider experience to the project. There is, however, a need to engender the commitment of the permanent staff so the team should not consist solely of external staff.

In theory, the grade of staff in the organizational review and teams should be less important than the skills they bring to the project. It may be necessary, however, to consider whether and how grade will affect the credibility and authority of the team in the eyes of other people in the organization. Many people will judge the status and importance of the project by the grade of those involved.

3.3.3 Skills and experience required

The people involved in re-organizing IT Services will need awareness and understanding of the following:

* the business processes and requirements of the parent organization

* IS strategy and implications for current and future service requirements

* experience in service design and process design

* the structure of the IT Directorate

* how business needs may be supported by IT

* IT service management

* the need for interfaces to people and groups outside IT Services

* management of change

* current trends in IT service management and staff organization.

The team's role will involve liaison throughout, and at all levels of, the organization so communication and inter-personal skills will be fundamental.

3.4   Timing

The timing of the review and any change will depend upon the reasons for review (such as change to Executive Agency status, introduction of new services, takeover or merger with other organizations). Timescales will depend upon available resources, pace of change, the needs of customers and the complexity and scale of change. Within the project plan timescales for key milestones may coincide with time factors such as financial year end or the need to reduce the number of staff by a given date.

Care needs to be taken if re-structuring of IT Services is part of a wider ranging project. Plans for IT Services must be considered in relation to any other organizational reviews taking place in the IT Directorate or parent organization.

4. Implementation

4.1 Procedures

The objective of the implementation phase is to carry out the planned changes in a controlled manner. This involves:

* finalizing implementation plans

* ensuring formal approval of plans and agreement to implement them (usually this will come from the IT Director)

* implementing the planned changes

* finalizing staff recruitment and training

* managing change.

Implementation may consist of several phases.

4.1.1 Finalize implementation plans

If there has been any delay between the planning and implementation phases there may be a need to confirm the implementation plan. Any changes to the assumptions on which the plan was prepared need to be examined and their implications assessed.

In major re-organizations the impact of variances within one sub-project need to be examined in respect of any dependent sub-projects.

4.1.2 Approval of plans

The organizational design and implementation plan must have appropriate management approval. Usually this will come from the IT Director but there may also be a need to obtain approval from managers or directors in the parent organization.

4.1.3 Implement the planned changes

The planned changes should be implemented in accordance with the plan and priorities.

Changes in organizational structure and responsibilities must be carried out with minimal risk to the continuing provision of existing services. It is not acceptable to customers for services to be disrupted due to organizational change within the IT Services Organization.

It is possible that in restructuring the organization and changing responsibilities some tasks may be overlooked despite careful planning. Managers need to be ready for this and prepared to act quickly; if necessary by allocating responsibilities on a temporary basis.

4.1.4 Finalize staff recruitment and training

Any necessary recruitment or training should be carried out in accordance with organizational policies before a new structure is implemented. Recruitment and training progress should be monitored against plans.

4.1.5 Managing Change

The need to manage the change process is often overlooked or considered only at the last minute. Although managing change is, for the sake of convenience, covered here under implementation, all the issues raised will need to have been taken into account from the outset of the project. The following sections indicate some management of change issues which will need to be addressed.

Understanding the organization and its culture

A thorough understanding of how the organization operates and of its strengths and weaknesses is required. This can be achieved through questionnaires and interviews with customers and internal staff.

The organization's culture, "the way we do things around here", may need to adapt to new ways of working. Changing culture (becoming more customer oriented, or operating as a business, for example) is always difficult. Knowing the organization's capability to respond is a critical factor in deciding whether the changes can be coped with and how they should be handled.

Managing communications

Communication is vital to the change process and helps the management of expectations. Information about the progress of the project should be issued on a regular basis to all people who are affected by the change. Involving staff and asking their views on the current situation or proposals is more likely to engender support than keeping staff in the dark.

Customers will also need to be informed of any changes in contacts or of location, for example if they are in future to contact the central, instead of a local, Help Desk.

Mechanisms that may assist communications include newsletters, bulletin boards, meetings, and the appointment of communications officers.

Changing the IT Services Organization will have an impact on many people inside and outside IT Services. The need for change must be understood and accepted throughout the organization if a return to old habits and practices is to be avoided.

This is particularly important when there is to be a change in the way customer liaison and support is carried out, or if there are to be newly formalized approaches to, say, change management. If previously informal routes to technical support are to be replaced by more formal Help Desk procedures, for example, both customers and IT staff must understand why.

Publishing plans helps reduce surprises while people should be clear what is expected of them to assist with planned changes. Both over and under expectation can be the source of demoralization, so efforts should be made to ensure expectations of the effect of change are realistic.

The planned organizational structure, implementation and resource plans should be published and formal briefings to IT Services staff held to explain the objectives of the re-structuring exercise, and their part in the project.

If there are to be staff cuts or a re-location, it is particularly important to involve personnel departments, Trades Unions (staff associations) and welfare services.

Making things happen

Setting up a team with specific responsibilities for a change programme, managed by someone with commitment and appropriate authority, will help ensure that change happens. This may or may not involve the same people as the organizational review, but the IT Director, IT Services Manager and other senior managers must be seen fully to support planned changes. The greater the change the greater is the investment of time and effort required. If motivation is lacking or if people see no benefit, change is unlikely to meet its objectives.

Where culture change is concerned, the new behaviours and values must be spelled out explicitly. People must be trained in new ways of working and those new ways must be rewarded and sustained. Otherwise it is likely that staff and customers will quickly revert to previous ways of working.

Supporting the people in the organization

Changing IT Services may mean new tasks, new skills, new tools and different ways of working. Training and development should focus on helping people to do their present job and enabling them to do new ones. Staff should be fully trained before taking on new responsibilities.

Staff may perceive organizational change as an opportunity or a threat. Threats may include loss of status, loss of overtime opportunities, the need to adopt different roles. These factors must be tackled openly and honestly. Opportunities may include new challenges, an opportunity to learn new skills and broaden experience. Benefits must be explained to everybody affected by any change.

Participation by all members of staff in discussions, workshops and presentations will facilitate the change process.

4.2 Dependencies

Implementation dependencies include:

* commitment from the IT Director, IT Services Organization staff and from other relevant senior managers

* willingness and ability of staff to change

* the impact and reasons for the change being understood by those who will be affected

* staff being available (in new locations if appropriate) and having been trained on time

* all job descriptions having been produced and new responsibilities understood

* interdependencies between service management functions being understood and addressed

* interfaces with other parts of the IT Directorate and the parent organization being understood and any changes agreed

* requirements for hardware and software having been met or will be met as planned

* accommodation requirements having been met.

4.3 People

Overall responsibility for implementing the organization structure and any revised practices rests with the IT Services Manager and in turn with the IT Director. Members of the IT Services management team or function managers should take responsibility for changes to their areas. Changes need to be 'championed' by managers who are committed to the new ways of working and are prepared to lend their effort and authority to making sure the change is successful.

The role of the organizational review team during implementation is likely to be one of coordination or provision of advice, ensuring that the rationale for any changes is understood.

4.4 Timing

Implementation should be carried out in line with customer priorities, commitments and resource availability. Periods when there is a lot of time-critical work (such as end of financial year) should, if possible, be avoided to reduce risk of changes to IT Services damaging the business.

An assessment of risks to the project should be made to identify threats to targets and timescales (such as the lack of trained staff) along with an estimate of the likely impact.

It will be necessary to balance the advantages and disadvantages of changing IT Services at the same time as other changes are taking place. If many changes are taking place at once there is a risk of instability, or of staff losing enthusiasm in the face of a deluge of changes. On the other hand there may be advantages of using one change to carry through another - getting all the changes out of the way in a shorter period can be less unsettling than a protracted series of smaller scale changes. Events such as the installation of new hardware platforms may provide an opportunity to introduce organizational changes.

5.   Post-implementation and audit

5.1   Procedures

Once a revised organizational structure has been implemented a Project Evaluation Review (PER) should be carried out. This will review the change project along the following lines:

* achievement against planned targets and critical success factors

* whether timescales and resource targets were met

* lessons to be learned from the conduct of the project.

When sufficient time has elapsed to assess the success (or otherwise) of the changes - ie the impact of the change project measured against the declared objectives - a Post Implementation Review (PIR) should take place.

The Post Implementation Review (PIR) provides a formal mechanism to assess the outcome of the changes, whether objectives have been met and expected benefits realized. For example the PIR may assess:

* whether the new structure adequately supports the provision of services which meet customer needs

* relationships with the rest of the IT Directorate

* whether costs have been reduced or value improved.

Change, however necessary, is unsettling and periods of change can, in the short term, reduce the organization's overall effectiveness if people have to learn new skills. Ideally a period of time, say six to twelve months, should be allowed following any major re-organization to allow for the new structure to settle down before further changes are considered. This may not, however, be possible if further changes are needed urgently or if new organizational problems have emerged.

Ongoing review

There is also a need for continuing review of the IT Services Organization to assess effectiveness and efficiency. The business environment is continually changing and review, at least of an informal kind, should be an ongoing activity. Changes in the business environment, trends and new pressures, should be monitored, and may indicate the need for a more formal review.

Direct measures of organizational effectiveness are difficult to define. The overall effectiveness of the IT Services Organization is, however, indicated by its ability to meet Service Level Agreements with customers.

A sound planning and control system, as described in the **Planning and Control for IT Services** module, provides the information required to enable managers to assess effectiveness and efficiency. Although not all deviations from plan or failures to meet targets are connected with organizational issues, consolidating management reports will highlight areas where the IT Services Organization is not meeting expectations. These can then be investigated to identify whether organizational issues, such as poorly defined responsibilities and poor communications, are responsible.

Other modules in the IT Infrastructure Library recommend regular, formal reviews of specific service management processes and functions to assess efficiency and effectiveness. These reviews should be coordinated to enable an assessment of how the IT Services Organization is performing overall and to confirm whether the organizational structure continues to support the needs of the business. Reviews may, for example, cover:

* whether services are being delivered in accordance with SLAs

* the effectiveness of service management processes

* whether individual, and groups of, service management functions are performing effectively

* whether costs and resource usage are as planned

* the adequacy of information flows between functions and groups

* customer perceptions of the effectiveness and efficiency of the IT Services Organization.

The review should also identify any trends relevant to the way individual service management functions may be carried out in the future.

The importance of subjective opinions about the IT Services Organization should not be overlooked. An attempt must be made to measure customers' perceptions and to assess the relationship between the IT Services Organization and its customers.

Audit

Audits should be carried out in accordance with any quality management system (QMS) being used by the organization. It is beyond the scope of this module to discuss the details of a QMS and reference should be made to the Quality Library, and to the IT Infrastructure Library module **Quality Management for IT Services**.

Audits should be conducted by independent audit teams from outside of IT Services and are carried out in order to:

* determine the existence of adequate procedures

* determine compliance with those procedures

* recommend improvements to existing procedures

* recommend adoption of additional procedures.

Implementing a QMS usually requires the clear definition and documentation of organizational structure, roles and responsibilities. Quality audits will seek to ensure these are in place and up to date.

Audit requirements for specific service management functions are described in other modules of the IT Infrastructure Library. The IT Services Manager should ensure that audit of service management functions is coordinated.

5.2 Dependencies

Post Implementation Reviews depend on the prior definition of project objectives against which progress can be assessed.

Reviews of the efficiency and effectiveness of the IT Services Organization depend on the availability of relevant management information, provided through a sound planning and control system. In particular, the IT Services Organization must be clear about what it is to achieve; Service Level Agreements are the basis for this because they document what the IT Services Organization must deliver to the customer. Cost management procedures are required so that the costs involved in meeting those requirements can be properly identified.

5.3 People

Ongoing monitoring and review is part of general line management. Where more formal reviews are required, organizational review teams could be formed by:

* in-house teams of line managers

* external consultants

* the quality manager

* other in-house teams such as staff inspection units.

Findings and recommendations from the reviews should be delivered to the IT Services Manager and the IT Director.

Individual managers need to monitor new or revised functions and be sensitive to early customer reactions. Criticisms may lead to a need for improved awareness or tuning of the function.

Audits of procedures must be carried out by people who are independent of the area being audited. Indeed, in general, organizational reviews benefit from some input from external people. For a review of a single function or small group of functions, this might mean involving a manager from a different part of IT Services. For wider reviews of IT Services, other parts of the IT Directorate or the parent organization could be involved. Where possible, reviews should not be carried out solely by third parties. Using internal staff helps ensure local knowledge is input to the review, ensures liaison across parts of the organization, allows for the transfer of skills from the external people, and helps in securing commitment.

5.4 Timing

Project Evaluation Reviews can be carried out as soon as the project is completed. Post-Implementation Reviews need to allow sufficient time for changes in the organization to have an effect. Formal reviews of efficiency and effectiveness should be carried out regularly, say annually, but monitoring efficiency and effectiveness is an ongoing task.

Organizational reviews of IT Services as a whole are usually triggered by some kind of change in the business environment but consideration should be given to carrying out such reviews on a two to three yearly basis. Decisions to carry out organizational reviews at some other level, perhaps of the parent organization as a whole or of the IT Directorate, may encapsulate or trigger a review of IT Services.

Where an organization is using a Quality Management System (QMS), quality reviews and audits will be specified within the QMS documentation.

6. Benefits, costs and possible problems

6.1 Benefits

Businesses depend on IT. The IT Services Organization and the IT Directorate as a whole have a responsibility to deliver quality IT services which meet business needs. This module provides guidance on planning and establishing an IT Services Organization that best meets the requirements of the business. It provides a framework to help choose the most appropriate management structure and carry out any necessary change to IT Services. A planned approach to organizing IT Services will help ensure that the organizational structure and practices will meet the needs of customers, be appropriate to the business environment in which IT Services operates and represent value for money.

The overall benefit from a well designed IT Services Organization is in ensuring business areas receive services that match their requirements.

More specifically, an IT Services Organization should be judged against three main criteria:

* service

    - does it deliver the service required by the business to agreed standards?

    - are customers satisfied with the style and level of customer interaction?

* cost

    - are services delivered as economically and efficiently as possible?

* flexibility

    - can it respond to changes in current and future business needs?

The module emphasizes the need for IT Services to take the needs of its customers as the main driver for decisions about what services it should provide, what processes it should put in place as well as what organizational structure it should adopt. Establishing a structure which will support good communications with customers must be a prime aim of organizational design and IT Services Managers should stress the importance of front line staff (such as Help Desks, Service Level Managers, Account Managers).

The combined mechanism of continuous monitoring and periodic review should ensure that IT Services is fully responsive to a changing business environment.

6.2   Costs

The costs involved in establishing the desired organizational structure will depend on the degree of change. Typical costs in implementing the guidance given in this module include:

* the cost of internal staff involved in carrying out reviews, planning and managing change

* the cost of any external staff brought in to support the project

* recruitment and training

* accommodation.

If changes in the organizational structure will lead to reductions in staff numbers, redundancy costs must also be considered.

Information about likely areas of cost related to implementing particular functions can be found in relevant IT Infrastructure Library modules.

6.3   Possible problems

Possible problems include:

* inadequate management leadership which may lead to inertia, conflict between factions in the organization and lack of confidence in the project plan

* failure to manage customer, staff or senior management expectations

* insufficient planning leading to unclear roles and responsibilities, inconsistent decisions, deviation from the project plan

* maintaining existing services whilst re-organizing

* incorrectly assessing skills requirements or skills availability

* fear of job losses, reluctance to change, apathy or inertia, all of which may threaten any required organizational changes

* obtaining the resources required to carry out organizational reviews and change programmes.

Throughout the project, planning, communication and effective management of change are keys to success. Communication should involve both customers and staff. If possible, staff involved in planning and implementing the new structure should be removed from the day-to-day delivery of services. Awareness campaigns should reflect the true nature of the change and should be realistic about its anticipated benefits.

7. Tools

Software tools which enable the introduction, or improve the efficiency and effectiveness, of specific service management functions are described in other IT Infrastructure Library modules.

Other tools which may be useful during organizational review and change projects include:

* planning and control tools

* reporting tools including statistics and graphics facilities, and spreadsheets

* project management tools.

Tools to help keep people informed include electronic mail, personal development plans for incorporating individuals into the project plan and personnel development schemes for planning the management of the change process.

Organizational design must take into account opportunities to support information flows, common information sources or requirements and linked procedures, through the use of software tools and shared databases.

The use of common software tools to support several service management functions can help integrate functions and remove the need for repeated collection and input of data, so improving efficiency. The use of a configuration management database (see the **Configuration Management** module) to underpin service support functions - comprising configuration management, change management, problem management, software control and distribution, and Help Desk functions - is one example. Further guidance is provided in the CCTA volume **IT Infrastructure Support Tools**.

More details about information flows between service management functions can be found in the **Planning and Control for IT Services** module.

A number of companies offer tools and schemes for comparing the operation and performance of an organization's IT Directorate against that of similar organizations. This usually involves payment of some form of membership fee and a charge for each evaluation exercise. Evaluations can concentrate on particular aspects of the IT Directorate. Such exercises are unlikely to provide

definitive answers about the organization of the IT
Directorate, but they may help identify areas where costs
are unusually high or which would otherwise merit further
investigation.

8. Bibliography

IS Guide E4 - Facilities Management (CCTA: John Wiley 1989 - ISBN 0 471 92547 0)

Prioritization (CCTA IS Planning Subject Guide 1992 - ISBN 0 946683 44 1)

The Role of the IT Planning Unit (CCTA IS Planning Subject Guide 1991 - ISBN 0 946683 42 5)

Prince in Small non-IT Projects (CCTA: HMSO 1990 - ISBN 0 11 330543 5)

The Intelligent Customer (CCTA 1993 - ISBN 0 946683 64 6)

The In-house Bid (CCTA Market Testing IS/IT booklet 1993)

Change for the Better? (CCTA Management Briefing 1992)

Guidance on the Grading of Posts in the IT Functional Specialism (available, for UK Government only, from HM Treasury)

Quality Management Library (CCTA: HMSO 1992 - ISBN 0 11 330569 9)

British Computer Society Industry Structure Model: Release 2
(British Computer Society 1991 - ISBN 0 901865 57 5)

Annex A.   Glossary of terms

Acronyms used in this module

BCS	British Computer Society
CAB	Change Advisory Board
CCTA	The Government Centre for Information Systems
CI	Configuration Item
CMDB	Configuration Management Database
DSL	Definitive Software Library
FM	Facilities Management
IS	Information Systems
ISM	Industry Structure Model (British Computer Society)
ISO	International Standards Organisation
ISPS	IS Planning Secretariat
ISSC	IS Steering Committee
IT	Information Technology
ITEC	IT Executive Committee
ITPU	IT Planning Unit
LAN	Local Area Network
LSA	Local Systems Administrator
NSM	Network Services Management
PC	Personal Computer
PDS	Professional Development Scheme (run by the British Computer Society)
PER	Project Evaluation Review
PIR	Post Implementation Review
PRINCE	PRojects IN Controlled Environments
QMS	Quality Management System
RFC	Request for Change
SC&D	Software Control and Distribution
SCT	Service Control Team
SLA	Service Level Agreement

Terms used in this module

Business Area	A discrete part of an organization that is managed as a single cohesive business or a related set of businesses that exhibit common business needs.
Contracting out	The process of buying in services, which were previously provided in-house, from a third party. In IS/IT terms it encompasses concepts such as facilities management, outsourcing, turnkey etc.
Customer	Taken to mean customers of IT Services or of the IT Directorate. In most cases customers are staff within business areas although software development and maintenance staff may also be customers of IT Services. The term is not used to mean customers in the wider sense, such as the general public in the case of many government departments.
Facilities Management	The provision of the management, and operation of an organization's computers and/or networks by an external source at agreed service levels. The service will generally be provided for a set time at an agreed cost.
Function	Within the IT Infrastructure Library a function is a logical set of tasks and activities, for example change management.
Infrastructure Management	The IT infrastructure consists of the hardware, software, computer related communications and documentation required to support the provision of IT services. Underpinning the IT infrastructure is the environmental infrastructure upon which it is built. These assets and their use must be managed, hence the term IT infrastructure management. IT infrastructure management is considered to be part of IT service management since it is an integral part of delivering IT services.
Intelligent Customer	The *intelligent customer* is a general description applied to an organization when its culture and procedures successfully enable the planning, implementation and use of IS/IT to achieve business objectives. A team is usually established to undertake the necessary activities.
IS Planning Secretariat	A central team providing support to the IS Steering Committee (ISSC) and coordinating the activities of the Executive Committee(s). The team is responsible for definition (in accordance with ISSC wishes), monitoring and review of the IS Strategy.

IT Planning Unit	A part of the IT Directorate, reporting both to the IT Director and to the IT Executive Committee. It coordinates the planning of the IT Directorate's activities as supplier of IT services to the organization, monitors achievement against plans and reviews plans. In particular, it draws up and is custodian of the IT Directorate's Tactical Plan.
IS Steering Committee	The top management group responsible for the direction of information systems. The ISSC commissions, directs and agrees the IS Strategy.
IT Executive Committee	The senior management group responsible for the executive coordination, control and direction of some or all of the IT projects that result from the IS strategy.
IT service	Within this module, taken to refer to operational IT services (rather than project or planning services). Operational IT services generally involve providing, operating and maintaining an IT infrastructure, and enabling access to information systems, applications and data.
IT Service Management	The totality of IT service provision and managing the IT infrastructure is referred to as IT service management (or simply service management). The terms IT systems management and IT service delivery are commonly used as well.
Market Testing	The process that allows in-house costs to be compared against those of the private sector based on commercial comparisons.
Matrix Management	A management approach whereby staff are managed by, or report to, more than one manager (typically a functional as well as a line manager, or process/product manager). For example Help Desk staff may be managed by the Problem Manager but also report to a Customer Liaison or Service Level Manager.
Outsourcing	See *contracting out*
Parent Organization	Within this module the parent organization is taken to be the wider business organization (for example a government department) of which the IT Directorate is a part along with the various business areas which are customers of IT Services.
Platform	The computer hardware, and the associated operating systems software necessary for its operation, on which applications software is run.

Project Support Office	A central support unit which provides a planning and monitoring service to project boards and project managers.
Role	A role indicates what is expected of a person in terms of activities and responsibilities. In this module the term is used to represent a logical concept. It is not synonymous with job since a person's job (what that person actually does or is responsible for) may combine several roles.
Service Control Team	A team of people with skills roughly equivalent to business analysts who will be responsible for managing an IS/IT provider on behalf of the customer organization.
Service Level Agreement	A written agreement between the customers and service provider which documents the agreed service levels for an IT service. Typically for an operational service it will cover: service hours, service availability, user support levels, throughputs and terminal response time, restrictions, functionality and the service levels to be provided in an emergency. It will also include security and accounting policy.
Service Management	see *IT Service Management*

Annex B. Functions covered by the IT Infrastructure Library

B.1   Introduction

This annex provides a brief description of the following service management functions, which are covered by the IT Infrastructure Library, to aid understanding of their value to the IT Services Organization:

* availability management

* capacity management

* change management

* computer operations management

* configuration management

* contingency planning

* cost management

* customer liaison

* environmental infrastructure management

* Help Desk

* management of local processors and terminals

* network services management

* operational testing

* problem management

* service level management

* software control and distribution

In addition, the following IT Infrastructure Library modules provide related guidance in support of these functions:

* Computer Installation and Acceptance

* Managing Supplier Relationships

* Planning and Control for IT services

* Quality Management for IT Services

* Software Lifecycle Support

* Third Party and Single Source Maintenance.

B.2 Availability management

Availability requirements will be specified in Service Level Agreements (SLAs). Availability management is concerned with optimizing the availability of IT services and the supporting IT infrastructure to ensure that customer requirements are met.

Availability management includes:

* advising the IT Directorate, service level management and application development teams on issues relating to availability to help ensure specified IT service requirements are realistic

* ensuring that the availability requirements of new services can be met and that those of existing services continue to be met

* monitoring availability, reliability, maintainability and serviceability of products and services from external suppliers to establish conformance to requirements

* improving availability beyond the required level within cost constraints.

Availability management contributes to service level management during service specification, design, development and delivery by providing availability data and forecasts.

B.3 Capacity management

Capacity management supports Service Level Management during the specification, design, development and delivery of IT services, by providing data and forecasts about the capacity of IT infrastructure components (including processing, storage, networking).

Capacity management includes:

* capacity planning - producing a plan of the IT resources which will be required to meet agreed service levels for performance and throughput up to the agreed planning horizon

* performance management - monitoring and tuning existing systems to ensure optimum use of IT resources and ensure service levels are maintained.

Accurately identifying capacity requirements will be essential to the proper functioning of the IT services.

**B.4 Change
management**

Planning, managing and controlling the implementation of
changes to any component of the IT infrastructure or to
procedures which affect the delivery of services is an
important part of configuration management (see below).

**B.5 Computer
operations
management**

Computer operations management is the organization and
conduct of computer operations to provide IT services
which meet Service Level Agreements

The nature of the IT service to be provided by operations
and the resources needed to do it are determined by the
contents of SLAs.

Operations staff must work closely with Help Desk and
problem management staff to handle IT service incidents.
Operations staff may be given devolved responsibility for
monitoring system performance, reporting on exceptions
and problems, and for day-to-day performance tuning
activities (see Capacity Management).

Computer operations management is complemented by
network services management.

Guidance on the use of automated and unattended
operations procedures is provided by the Unattended
Operating module.

**B.6 Configuration
management**

Configuration management (including change
management) is concerned with identifying, recording and
giving the organization control over its IT assets. Data is
usually held in a configuration management database.

Configuration management covers:

* identifying all components in an IT infrastructure

* controlling changes to the IT infrastructure

* recording and reporting current and historical data
about components in the IT infrastructure

* checking that physical components in the IT
infrastructure match records in the configuration
management database.

B.7 Contingency planning

Contingency planning is carried out to ensure that an agreed level of service is maintained in the event of a disaster or serious incident which would otherwise threaten partial or complete loss of service.

Contingency planning includes:

* producing a contingency plan based on perceived threats, vulnerabilities and contingency options

* reviewing, testing and maintaining the contingency plan.

Modified service levels which would apply when a contingency service is in operation, should be contained in Service Level Agreements.

B.8 Cost management

Cost management addresses the management accounting required for the IT Services Organization and the pricing of and charging for IT services if appropriate.

Pricing and charging policies will influence customer perception and use of the IT services provided. Service charges or cost allocations should be written into Service Level Agreements where appropriate.

B.9 Customer liaison

The customer liaison function is concerned with liaison, communication and ensuring co-operation between IT Services and its customers.

All staff who are involved with customers have a customer liaison responsibility. Help Desk staff in particular can make an important contribution to customer liaison. Account management, marketing and sales activities are also aspects of customer liaison.

Creating Customer Services groups may help provide a focus for customer liaison, bringing together staff with responsibilities for, eg, Help Desk, service level management and other customer oriented activities.

B.10 Environmental infrastructure management

Management of the office and computer centre environment underpins management of the IT infrastructure. Activities include:

* office design and planning

* establishing and implementing facilities to support requirements for power, cabling, lighting, fire prevention etc

* human factors in the office environment (such as ergonomics, job design, health, training)

* specifying requirements for computer centre design.

Responsibility for the environmental infrastructure is likely to be shared between the IT Services Organization, which has a particular interest in the environmental requirements of the IT infrastructure, and people with broader responsibilities for accommodation, office and management services.

B.11 Help Desk

The Help Desk is a vital part of the interface between the IT Services Organization and its customers. The Help Desk provides first level incident support, advice and acts as a day-to-day contact point for users of IT services.

The Help Desk also has an important role in providing reports on service quality.

Having responsibility for handling service incidents reported by customers, the Help Desk supports a significant part of the overall problem management system.

B.12 Management of local processors and terminals

Local processors and terminals which are physically located in the customer domain still need to be managed as part of the IT infrastructure. The IT Directorate can provide vital support through many of the IT infrastructure management functions such as Help Desk and Service Level Management, without impinging on the benefits of moving day-to-day control of a local IT service to the business customers.

However, it is important to agree the division of responsibility between the central (ie IT) and local (ie business) management for the provision of IT facilities within the business areas.

B.13 Network services management

Network services management (NSM) includes the planning, implementation and on-going management of network services, and networks. The responsibilities of an NSM function are split into four major parts:

* network services planning (strategic and tactical planning processes)

* network services administration (tactical planning and implementation of network equipment)

* network services control (day-to-day operation and control)

* network services project control (project management of major projects).

Network services should be managed as an integral part of the IT infrastructure and managers of network services and computer operations must work closely together to provide the services required and resolve service incidents and problems.

B.14 Operational testing

The role of operating testing is to ensure, as cost effectively as possible, that a new or revised IT service will support the business needs for which it has been developed and may be introduced with minimal risk to other services.

The **Testing an IT Service for Operational Use** module addresses the following:

* system testing - demonstrating that an IT service meets the agreed requirements under all operating conditions

* installation testing - showing that the IT service is correctly installed in its live environment and meets the requirements of computer operations staff

* acceptance testing - gaining acceptance from users that the installed IT service meets their requirements, in terms of usability as well as functionality.

Operational testing requires the involvement of a number of interested parties, including customers, software developers and maintainers, and a range of service management functions.

B.15 Problem management

Problem management is a discipline for handling all types of failures in IT services. It is concerned not only to minimize the impact of failures when they occur, but also to correct the root causes of service failures.

Problem management includes:

* incident control - restoring normal service when the service has gone wrong (usually centred on the Help Desk)

* problem control - getting to the root cause of incidents

* error control - correcting problems.

While they are both part of problem management, incident and problem control each have a different focus. The emphasis of incident control is in getting the service back to normal as quickly as possible rather than with identifying trends and underlying causes of incidents. It is often advantageous to separate these responsibilities.

Problem management requires collaboration with many parts of the IT Directorate, including computer and network operations staff, applications development and maintenance teams and technical support staff.

B.16 Service level management

Service level management is the process of defining, negotiating, contracting, monitoring and reviewing the levels of service that customers require. Service descriptions and service levels should be documented in Service Level Agreements (which may be embodied in contracts if services are provided externally).

Service level management is supported by the range of service management functions, each of which provides information to enable the specification, delivery and monitoring of IT services.

B.17 Software control and distribution

Software control and distribution involves controlling, storing, releasing, distributing and bringing into service authorized software. It may be considered as part of configuration management and is closely related to the testing of IT services.

Annex C.   Examples of IT Services Organizations

C.1   Introduction

This Annex provides several example structures for IT Services Organizations. These have been chosen for the way organizational structure has been influenced by combinations of factors such as:

* relationship with customers

* relationships with other parts of the IT Directorate

* nature of services provided

* degree to which IT resources and/or responsibilities are centralized

* size of user population

* degree of contracting out

* hardware and software platforms used.

It would not be possible to isolate the effects of each factor but for each example there is a discussion of the impact of the factors taken as a whole.

The examples are based on real organizational structures, although adjustments have been made for simplicity and clarity. Terms used for functions and roles have been standardized to some degree, to make it easier to compare examples.

The examples show the importance of the business environment. Some service management functions are particularly influenced by the way IT provision is approached in the parent organization as a whole or in the IT Directorate. Service management functions most directly affected are those concerned with:

* the customer interface (customer liaison, Help Desk, service level management, quality management for IT services)

* integrated planning (planning and control for IT services, network services management, capacity management, contingency planning, management of local processors and terminals)

* costing and charging (cost management).

In the public sector, market testing is having a significant effect on the organization of IT Services. In broad terms IT organizations facing market testing must look critically at costs and seek to minimize them. Reviews of the organization must focus on what functions, roles, skills and staff numbers are needed to deliver the services customers require.

Cost management is fundamental in organizations considering market testing, as each area to be market tested will need to be able to identify its own costs and to be able to charge for the services it provides.

A range of CCTA publications offers advice on the process and wider implications of market testing.

C.2   Example 1

In this example IT Services supports both central mainframe and distributed systems. IT Services has been organized into functional groups. Within both the Operations and Technical Services groups there are teams responsible for supporting particular software and hardware platforms with a common line of command.

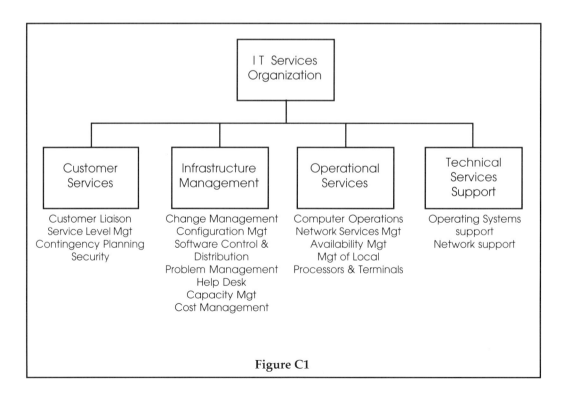

Figure C1

Customer Services and Infrastructure Management groups are formed on functional lines irrespective of technical platforms. The Help Desk forms part of the problem management line of command.

The Technical Services Support group includes staff responsible for networks and systems software support.

Security issues, including contingency planning, are a high priority and have high visibility within the Customer Services group. This helps ensure that security is driven from the customer's perspective.

C.3   Example 2

In this example a large IT Directorate provides a range of IT services to several customer groups.

Characteristics are:

*   the majority of services are provided on a single technical platform (centralized mainframes)

*   the workload has historically been fairly predictable (day-to-day running of large operational systems)

*   the customer groups supported are separate organizations

*   the IT Directorate increasingly must compete with external IT providers and operates on a commercial basis.

The need for cost-effectiveness across all its service streams is a major driver. Clear customer relationships and accountability for quality of services have led to the creation of an organization structure which emphasizes these aspects.

Most customer-facing functions have been placed in a marketing group which includes responsibilities for account management, negotiation of Service Level Agreements (SLAs) and marketing. Day-to-day monitoring of service levels is the responsibility of staff within the IT Services group.

Account Managers within the Customer Services group establish SLAs with customers and, as the owners of SLAs within the IT Directorate, in effect sub-contract with the IT Services Organization to deliver the service required to meet those SLAs. Account management aims to make a profit; the IT Services and software development groups must recover costs.

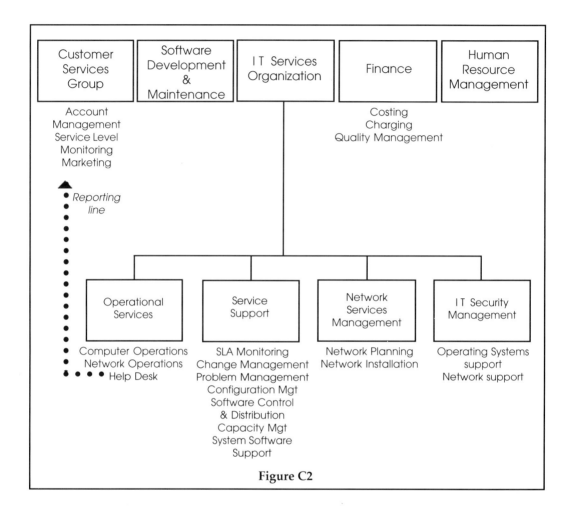

Figure C2

Costing and charging is coordinated through the Finance group, although each group must collect cost data.

The Help Desk, which has been placed within Operational Services, also has a reporting responsibility to the Customer Services group. It had been intended to place the Help Desk within the business management function to emphasize its customer facing role. It was decided, however, that because the Help Desk was heavily involved in day-to-day operational issues it could be managed from within Operational Services with a strong link to business management.

Capacity planning and performance monitoring are separate roles within Service Support.

C.4   Example 3

This example represents a very large IT Directorate supporting a range of business and administrative systems, on a number of distinct hardware and software platforms. Traditionally the IT Directorate was organized on the basis of separate structures for each platform but reorganizations have sought to improve communication and coordination, and to develop a more functionally-based structure.

Characteristics are:

* IT Services supports both central mainframes and distributed equipment

* several software and hardware platforms are supported (but moving towards using similar software and hardware platforms)

* a large customer base, geographically dispersed

* a need for clearly defined service areas for which costs can clearly be identified.

An increasing need to provide services which involve different platforms, along with the increased use of distributed systems and PCs, highlighted the need for a more functionally oriented structure. Other key pressures which led to a major organizational review included the need to reduce costs, reduce duplication of effort, enable a more strategic (because less platform driven) approach to planning and to prepare for possible market testing.

A range of objectives were identified for the review including improving communication, increasing flexibility in the use of resources, increasing consistency of management practice, reducing the number of management levels, and separating work and people management (so releasing technical staff from some line management duties).

Figure C3, overleaf, shows the organizational structure which resulted from the review.

Liaison with customers occurs at several levels. The Help Desk deals with the end-users of services; negotiations about Service Level Agreements involve the Business Support group; while high level liaison is channelled through the account management function.

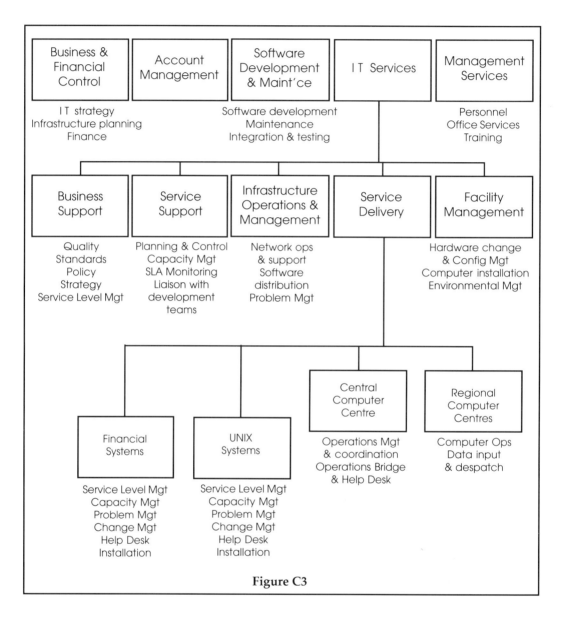

Figure C3

The central Help Desk is part of an Operations Bridge and is managed as part of the Service Delivery group. Regional support desks acting as filters, dealing with initial calls and with calls concerned with the operations of particular business systems, are gradually being phased out in favour of a centralized Help Desk which also deals with incidents. Incidents that cannot be resolved locally are passed to the central Help Desk.

The central computer centre provides central operations management and coordination of regional centres. Operation of regional computer centres is highly automated. Regional sites are responsible for local data input and output, and have a limited degree of flexibility in scheduling and running local systems.

In addition to the main central services, two sites support services which run on other platforms. To a large extent these have been seen as distinct services which support different groups of customers. As a result separate service management organizations have grown up, operating in a semi-autonomous way though under the general IT Services planning and management umbrella. These separate groups persist to a declining extent as the separation of services and customers on the basis of platforms becomes less appropriate.

The size and complexity of the IT infrastructure means there is a need for considerable liaison between functional groups, different technical groups and between staff in different locations. Therefore the organizational structure embodies and is supplemented by a number of mechanisms for coordination and liaison. Matrix management is operated in a number of areas. Resource managers are responsible for groups of technical staff, agreeing the allocation of resources with managers responsible for particular projects or services, and taking responsibility for longer term staff development.

C.5   Example 4

IT Services supports a customer base which is spread over a large number of locations. Services are provided on a number of platforms including mainframes and small systems.

Service management functions have been divided into two broad groups based on their different perspectives - planning and operations. The Service Operations group is responsible for all functions concerned with the day-to-day delivery of IT services including computer operations and network services management.

The Service Planning group brings together all planning responsibilities in the IT Services area (it is separate from planning the software development). Within Service Planning, specialist teams are responsible for particular technical environments (eg mainframe services, office systems, networks).

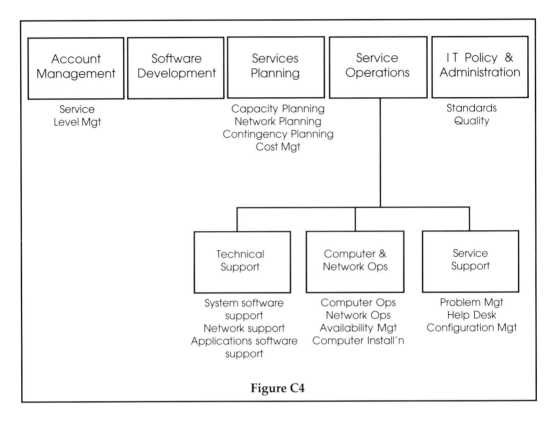

Figure C4

Account management provides a coordinated interface with customers for both ongoing service delivery and for software development. Support for strategy, programme and infrastructure planning is also provided by this group.

C.6   Example 5

This IT organization was restructured in advance of, and to prepare for, market testing. Characteristics were:

* a large user base, dispersed organizationally and geographically

* a central IT Directorate providing a number of large IT systems on a bureau basis from a single site

* a large number of small systems controlled by users running on stand-alone PCs or small LANs

* no overall IS strategy embracing the entire customer base, but a set of largely independent plans for the use of IS/IT relating to each of the main business areas.

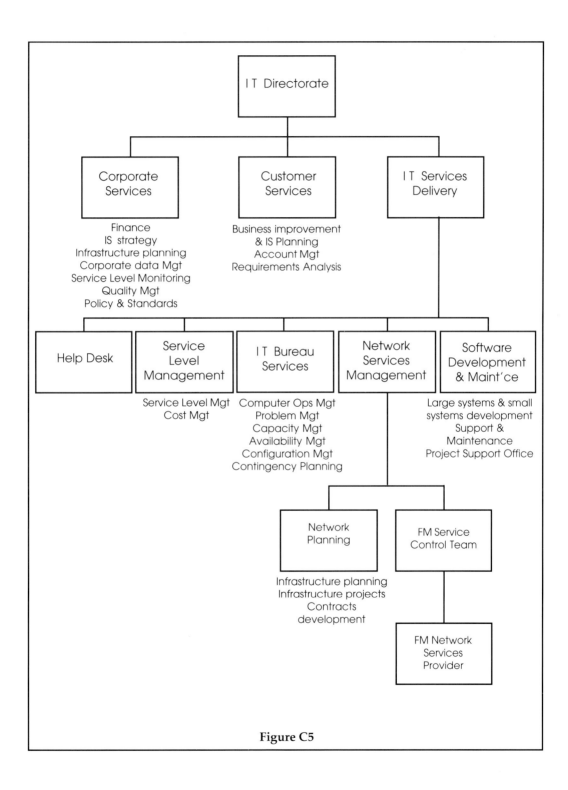

Figure C5

The services offered by the IT Directorate (small and larger systems development, Help Desk, the bureau and networking) were identified as likely candidates for market testing. There may be potential to move the Help Desk into the Customer Services group (or the Corporate Services function) should the centrally provided IT services be contracted out but the Help Desk stay in-house.

Corporate groups - Customer Services, and Corporate Services - provide the basis for a corporate *intelligent customer* function able to work on behalf of the disparate customers.

C.7   Example 6

This example is concerned less with the organization of functions within the IT Services Organization than with the impact of creating an *intelligent customer* function.

This impact is most marked where the parent organization consists of a number of autonomous business units, possibly Executive Agencies, and the IT Directorate (potentially an Agency in its own right) has the responsibility for providing coherent and cost-effective IT services shared by the business units.

Characteristics are:

* each business unit has developed and maintains its own IS strategy

* there is corporate concern to optimize shared facilities, systems, infrastructure and information

* financing of IT development and services is determined on a corporate (and then allocated) basis

* because of the extent of shared facilities and resources, value for money needs to be judged on a corporate basis.

In this scenario, particularly with recent and rapid changes to the accountability and freedoms of business units, there is often a need to establish a corporate *intelligent customer*.

Responsibilities of the *intelligent customer* function include:

* development and maintenance of IT infrastructure strategy and plans

* coordination of business unit IS strategies and plans and the negotiation of IT work programmes

* IT related management and technical policies including procurement

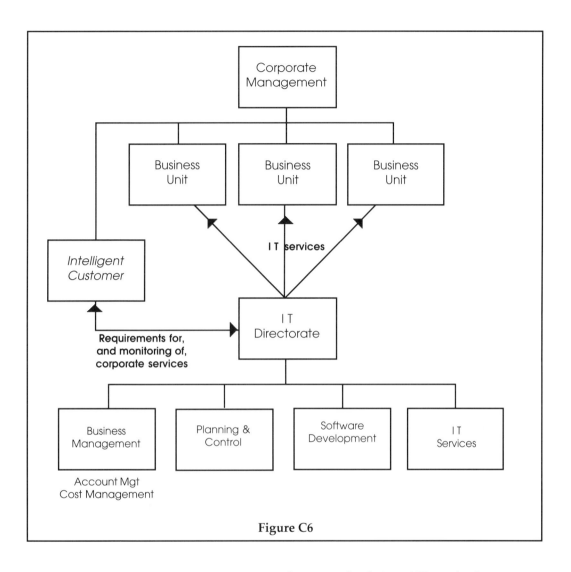

Figure C6

* promulgation and policing of IT standards

* procurement of IT services (including those from the in-house IT organization)

* data management

* assurance of value for money from IT services provision and potentially the running of any market testing process

* management of contracts for IT services on a corporate basis.

As guardian of the infrastructure strategy and associated programmes the intelligent customer function is the corporate customer for infrastructure development. Business areas are customers for particular services.

Coordination and consolidation of business units' IT strategies is carried out by the *intelligent customer* function. The IT Directorate must develop an overall IT resource plan, to identify the resources required by the IT Directorate in order to meet those consolidated requirements.

Annex D.   Example Role Descriptions

This annex provides role descriptions for managers of core service management functions. They should be seen as guides to the responsibilities related to each service management function but are not intended to be prescriptive.

The following role descriptions are included:

* IT Services Manager (see D1)

* Availability Manager (see D2)

* Capacity Manager (see D3)

* Change Manager (see D4)

* Computer Operations Manager (see D5)

* Configuration Manager (see D6)

* Contingency Planning Manager (see D7)

* Cost Manager (see D8)

* Customer Liaison Manager (see D9)

* Manager for Local Processors and Terminals (see D10)

* Local Systems Administrator (see D11)

* Network Services Manager (see D12)

* Problem Manager (see D13)

* Service Level Manager (see D14)

* Software Control and Distribution Manager (see D15)

* Operational Test Manager (see D16)

* Supplier Manager (see D17)

* IT Services Coordinator (see D18)

* IT Security Manager (D19)

* IT Services Planning and Control Manager (see D20).

Roles related to management of the environmental infrastructure are not included.

A possible template for addressing staff and skill needs within IT Services is the British Computer Society (BCS) Industry Structure Model (ISM), which underpins the BCS Professional Development Scheme. The BCS ISM provides a neutral basis for deciding grades of staff, identifying skills profiles and likely levels of experience, and responsibility for various roles. Likely levels for most IT Services functions covered by this module are levels six to eight. These are described by the BCS as being:

* Level 6 - Specialist Practitioner/Manager (limited scope) - the level associated with a fully experienced information systems professional carrying full responsibility for defined areas of activity usually in a specialist, consultant or management capacity.

* Level 7 - Senior Specialist/Manager (extended scope) - the level where the focus of activity is either on function management (not necessarily related to a purely technical role) or alternatively the acceptance of professional responsibility at a senior level calling for a wide and deep specialized information systems knowledge.

* Level 8 - Principal Specialist/Experienced Manager - the upper of two levels where the focus of activity is either on function management (not necessarily related to a purely technical role) or alternatively the acceptance of professional responsibility at a senior level calling for a wide and deep specialized information systems knowledge.

It is assumed that there is no level nine post within IT Services, since this is the potential level of the IT Director.

More information about the BCS Professional Development Scheme and the Industry Structure Model can be obtained from:

The PDS Department
The British Computer Society
PO Box 1454
Station Road
Swindon
SN1 1TG.

The following descriptions briefly cover the responsibility of the role and the major tasks. Where applicable a cross-reference is given to the BCS model as a guide to likely skills required.

D.1 IT Services Manager

Responsibilities

The IT Services Manager is the head of IT Services and has overall responsibility to the IT Director for service quality.

The IT Services Manager may have the added responsibility for business management related functions such as Account Management.

Tasks

The IT Services Manager:

* heads the IT Services management team

* ensures the efficient delivery of cost-effective, quality services to customers and users

* has overall responsibility for IT Services Organization plans and budgets

* represents IT Services to the IT Director and senior non-IT management

* has overall responsibility for review of progress and status against plans produced, and for reporting this to the IT Director

* acts as the primary interface for incoming requirements from programme and project plans

* acts as the primary interface for arranging IT Services' input and advice to other groups

* defines the lines of responsibility for the individual functions which compose IT Services

* agrees staffing levels with managers of service management functions and thereafter negotiates with the IT Director about staffing and recruitment

* ensures that delivered systems meet acceptance criteria and that such systems are capable of meeting Service Level Agreements.

BCS ISM Cross-reference

See BCS model cell reference OPM8 (Service Delivery Management substream).

D.2 Availability Manager

Responsibilities

The Availability Manager is responsible for ensuring availability requirements are met and for advising senior IT management accordingly.

Tasks

The Availability Manager:

* specifies and maintains all procedures required for the availability management function

* supervises the collection of reliability, maintainability and serviceability data on all configuration items (from hardware monitors and from company statistics)

* produces the availability report

* assesses the impact of Requests for Change on availability and attends Change Advisory Board (CAB) meetings when appropriate

* is responsible for ensuring that the availability criteria of Service Level Agreements are met

* publicizes the availability management function and ensures that all relevant staff are familiar with procedures

* analyzes and reviews the availability management function on a regular basis to ensure its effectiveness and efficiency, plans for audits, recommends improvements where needed

* is a member of the Planning and Control Team

* produces and publishes the Availability Plan discussing the ability of the IT infrastructure to meet the availability requirements of the business

* is responsible for initiating changes to ensure that availability requirements are met and to improve availability beyond the required level within cost constraints

* is responsible for monitoring compliance of IT suppliers to contractual conditions and participates in the negotiation and management of contracts to underpin the Service Level Agreements

* advises the IT Directorate, the Service Level Manager and applications development teams on issues regarding availability

* ensures that availability requirements of new IT services can be met by determining the reliability, maintainability and serviceability requirements from the design

* advises on the availability requirements of new services in relation to obtaining the proper cost/ quality balance

* maintains an awareness of advances in availability management eg new tools produced.

BCS ISM Cross-reference

There is no direct comparison within the BCS model. The skills needed by the Availability Manager, beyond those of any other management position, are a blend of those needed by the Service Level Manager and Capacity Manager. Reference should be made to BCS model cell references USM6 and OPT6 (Service Level Management, Capacity and Performance Specialism, substreams).

D.3 Capacity Manager

Responsibilities

The Capacity Manager has overall responsibility for ensuring that there is adequate IT capacity to meet required levels of service and for ensuring that senior IT management is correctly advised on how to match capacity and demand, and ensure that use of existing capacity is optimized.

The Capacity Manager is also responsible for advising the Service Level Manager about appropriate service levels or service level options.

Tasks

The Capacity Manager:

* produces capacity plans in line the organization business planning cycle, identifying capacity requirements early enough to take account of procurement lead times; documents the need for any hardware upgrades or additional equipment based on service level requirements and cost constraints

* is a member of the Planning and Control Team

* produces regular management reports which include current usage of resources, trends and forecasts

* sizes all proposed new systems, including for example, bespoke applications, packages, decision support systems and office systems with respect to the computer and network resources required, to determine hardware utilizations, performance service levels and cost implications

* assesses new technology and its relevance to the organization in terms of performance and cost

* implements a service level reporting system

* maintains a knowledge of future demand for IT services and predicts the effects of demand on performance service levels

* determines performance service levels that are maintainable and cost justified

* carries out performance testing of new systems

* recommends tuning of systems and makes recommendations to IT management on the design and use of systems to help ensure optimum use of all hardware and operating software resources

* recommends resolutions to performance problems

* recommends to IT services management when to employ demand management techniques (to dampen customer demands on the systems)

* carries out ad hoc studies in the area of capacity management on request from IT Management

* ensures requirements for reliability and availability are taken into account in all capacity planning and sizing activity.

BCS ISM Cross-reference

See BCS model code OPT6/7 (Capacity and Performance Specialism substream).

Note

If a separate Network Capacity Manager is to be appointed it should normally be a computer literate person with extensive telecommunications experience, or a telecommunications literate person with extensive computer experience. The job has a high technical and analytical content and may require management of a small

team of technical specialists. To this extent, the
qualifications and experience required are similar to those
of a computer systems-programming team leader. Indeed,
this may be seen as a career move for network systems
programmers or for particularly able network operations
personnel.

D.4   Change Manager

Responsibilities

The Change Manager is responsible for the control of the
change management mechanism.

Tasks

The Change Manager:

*   is responsible for ensuring Requests for Change
    (RFCs) are received, logged and allocated priority in
    collaboration with the initiator, while rejecting any
    RFCs that are impractical

*   tables all non-urgent RFCs for a Change Advisory
    Board (CAB) meeting, issues agenda and circulates
    all RFCs to CAB members in advance of meetings to
    allow prior consideration; convenes an urgent CAB
    meeting for all urgent RFCs

*   chairs all CAB meetings. After consideration of the
    advice given by the CAB the Change Manager
    authorizes those changes that are acceptable and
    issues forward schedules of changes via the Help
    Desk

*   liaises with all necessary parties to coordinate change
    building, testing and implementation, in accordance
    with schedules. Updates change log with all progress
    that occurs, including any actions to correct
    problems and/or to take opportunities to improve IT
    service quality

*   reviews all implemented changes to ensure that they
    have met their objectives. Refers-back any that have
    been unsuccessful

*   reviews all outstanding RFCs awaiting consideration
    or awaiting action

*   analyzes change records to determine any trends or
    apparent problems that occur. Seeks rectification
    with relevant parties

*   produces regular and accurate management reports.

BCS ISM Cross-reference

The skills need by the Change Manager are a blend of those found in the BCS model cell codes OPB6 and OPM6 (Problem Management and Service Delivery Management substreams).

D.5 Computer Operations Manager

Responsibilities

The Operations Manager is responsible for setting up and managing a computer operation, supported by other IT service management disciplines, that is responsible for operating computers in such a way that IT services can be delivered to the level of quality required in the current and future Service Level Agreements.

Tasks

The Operations Manager:

* directs and administers the Operations area production process to meet production targets

* develops and maintains controls and procedures to ensure that the Operations production process runs efficiently, ensuring in the event of failure that Operations staff can recover the operation in accordance with a predefined and tested recovery or contingency plan, to maintain an agreed fallback level of service within a set time

* produces resource usage measures for customer cost allocation

* is a member of the Planning and Control Team

* plans and oversees the installation of computer hardware and liaises regularly with supplier staff to ensure adequate support is provided

* ensures that the physical environment is maintained and secure according to contractual requirements and business needs

* ensures that the Operations budget is managed within the financial limits agreed

* ensures that new production systems meet the agreed operability criteria for live running prior to accepting them

* ensures that the IT Services Manager is provided with regular feedback on Operations performance

* ensures that all contractual documentation relevant to maintenance contracts is complete.

BCS ISM Cross-reference

See BCS model code OPC6 (Operations Command substream).

D.6 Configuration Manager

Responsibilities

The Configuration Manager is responsible for managing the configuration management system and bringing all IT infrastructure components under configuration management control.

Tasks

The Configuration Manager:

* agrees overall objectives for configuration management with the IT Services Manager

* mounts awareness campaigns to win support for configuration management procedures

* proposes and agrees scope of configuration management function, items that are to be controlled, and information that is to be recorded

* proposes and agrees level at which configuration items (CIs) are to be identified

* proposes and agrees naming and numbering conventions

* establishes and implements CI registration procedures

* evaluates and arranges for procurement of support tools

* proposes and/or agrees interfaces with change management, problem management, computer operations, network services management, software control and distribution, and finance and administration functions

* plans, publicizes and oversees implementation of new configuration management functions

* plans and executes population of the configuration management database (CMDB)

* uses or provides CMDB to facilitate impact assessment for Requests for Change

* uses or provides CMDB to help identify the other CIs affected by a fault that is affecting a CI

* creates change records, package release records to specify the effect on CIs of an authorized change

* uses the CMDB to ensure implemented changes are as authorized

* updates the CMDB when a change is implemented to record the effects on the IT infrastructure of the change

* ensures any changes to authorized records are themselves subject to change management

* frequently checks that the physical IT inventory is consistent with the CMDB and instigates any necessary corrective action

* ensures regular housekeeping of the CMDB - continually plans for growth and change

* instigates any action needed to secure funds and enhance the IT infrastructure and staffing levels to cope with growth and change

* continually reviews the configuration management function for efficiency and effectiveness

* assists auditors to audit the activities of the configuration management team for compliance to laid down procedures and ensures that any remaining corrective action is carried out

* ensures regular production of management reports, indicating suggested action to deal with any current or foreseen shortcomings.

BCS ISM Cross-reference

See BCS model cell ref OPA6-7 (IS Asset Control Specialism substream).

D.7 Contingency Planning Manager

Responsibilities

The Contingency Planning Manager is responsible for the creation and maintenance of the Contingency Plan required to recover the agreed level of service in the event of a contingency.

Tasks

The Contingency Planning Manager:

* is responsible for the planning, production and testing of the Contingency Plan

* reviews the Contingency Plan regularly, at least every 6 months, in collaboration with customers; after the annual test; following an actual disaster

* keeps the Plan up to date by referring to

 - information on all IT changes (via the Change Management system)

 - other relevant organizational changes eg. accommodation

 - IT strategy changes

* understands and applies any relevant guidelines or standards to the contingency plans produced within IT Services.

BCS ISM Cross-reference

See BCS model code ISS6 (Security and Contingency Planning specialism substream).

D.8 Cost Manager

Responsibilities

The Cost Manager has responsibility for the overall running of the cost management system.

Tasks

The Cost Manager:

* specifies, initiates and maintains the cost management system and information structure including cost centres, classifications of workload and equipment requirements as described in the **Cost Management for IT Services** module

* supervises the collation of all costs associated with the provision of IT services

* is responsible for the production of cost recovery plans and charging algorithms (where appropriate)

* supervises the monitoring of IT service costs to ensure that business objectives (including the creation of projects from IT service provision, where appropriate) are achieved

* publicizes the cost management system to the organization, ensures that all IT Service Organization staff are familiar with procedures and are satisfied with the day-to-day operation of the system

* analyzes and reviews the cost management system on a regular basis to ensure its effectiveness and to recommend improvements where needed

* attends Change Advisory Board (CAB) meetings

* produces regular reports about the effectiveness of the system for the IT Directorate

* is responsible for preparing the cost management sections of IT strategic and tactical plans.

BCS ISM Cross-reference

The skills of Cost Manager need to reflect an understanding of the supply of IT resources and the wider aspects of IT service delivery. The skills therefore are likely to be a blend of BCS ISM cell references OPM6 (Service Delivery Management substream)and OPT5/6 (Capacity and Performance Specialism substream).

D.9 Customer Liaison Manager

Responsibilities

To ensure that by effective liaison, IT Services provides its customers with the support necessary to enable them to use IT services effectively and efficiently, whilst making the most efficient use of IT resources.

Tasks

The Customer Liaison Manager:

* provides quality support to all customers of IT Services by

  - advising and assisting IT customers to make best use of IT services and jointly determining (in line with strategies and plans) future uses to help customers derive maximum benefit

  - ensuring that IT providers are aware of customers' views and bear them in mind during the planning and provision of services

* ensures customer complaints are followed-up promptly and encourages customers to participate in achieving ongoing improvement in the services provided to them

* ensures that standard procedures and good practices are used in all contacts between IT Services and its customers

* regularly monitors customers' perceptions of the IT service offered and the level of satisfaction, and instigates improvements to tackle deficiencies

* sets up means of improving service to and relationships with customers by

  - appointing task teams to attend to specific problems

  - encouraging the formation of 'customer groups'

  - improving communications

* seeks to bring about greater awareness amongst IT Services staff of the need to achieve and maintain quality customer service by different methods of communication and training

* initiates projects, as agreed by IT management, aimed at ensuring overall improvements in IT Services /customer relationships (for example a customer care programme).

BCS ISM Cross-reference

The BCS model has a category of roles, ranging from level 1 to level 5, defined as Customer/User support (USP1-5). At the highest level, the responsibility and tasks described are quite well aligned to the customer support role of the Customer Liaison Manager but do not cover his/her tasks to promote awareness within IT Services of the need to achieve and maintain quality customer service and to proactively work towards this. These aspects are however covered to a certain extent by some of the tasks/attributes of the BCS model role of Service Delivery Management (OPM6).

The Customer Liaison Manager has a wide ranging remit and therefore needs to be well skilled in customer care and have extensive knowledge of the detailed provision of quality IT services.

Where business management functions subsume those of customer liaison then the management role should incorporate BCS cell references SMS8 (IS Sales specialism) and SMM7 (IS Marketing specialism).

D.10 Manager for Local Processors and Terminals

Responsibilities

The Manager for Local Processors and Terminals is responsible for coordinating, controlling and supporting IT equipment sited in the customer domain, for which IT Services has central responsibility.

Tasks

The Manager for Local Processors and Terminals:

* supports customers in the use and management of their local processors and terminals, in line with Service Level Agreements (SLAs)

* maintains day-to-day communications with customers and other IT staff, and identifies any factors which might affect the continued relevance or attainment of SLAs

* advises customers on suitable use of IT services in addressing their business requirements, and the formulation of requests for procuring hardware, software and services in line with standards

    * maintains an awareness of relevant products and practices within the customer environment, and provides the coordination necessary to ensure that services are controlled in a manner that is secure, cost-effective, and compliant with legal and industrial relations requirements

    * ensures that local systems comply with organization and system security policies and procedures, including

       - password mechanisms

       - combating viruses

       - authorized software

    * develops a perspective of both organizational directions and developments within the IT industry, so as to be able to assist in the formulation of business and communications IS strategies

    * recruits and develops an organization to meet the above accountabilities

    * acts as technical manager for Local Systems Administrators (LSAs) including

       - assisting customer departments with selection and appointment

       - ensuring technical training is supplied

       - monitoring the technical competence and performance of LSAs.

BCS ISM Cross-reference

No relevant cross-reference.

D.11 Local Systems Administrator

Responsibilities

The Local Systems Administrator (LSA) is responsible for IT equipment and services located within one or more business communities. The LSA will normally be a member of the business community with normal line management supplemented by technical management exercised by the Manager for Local Processors and Terminals.

Tasks

The Local Systems Administrator:

* is responsible for the smooth running of the managed local IT services in keeping with Service Level Agreements (SLAs)

* protects the integrity of data relating to the supported services, taking backups as necessary and arranges for their secure storage, liaising with database coordinators as required

* controls access to programs and to data files and other machine resources to customers on a basis of operational necessity

* acts as the local coordination point for reporting incidents to the Help Desk. Reports all such incidents to the central Help Desk, including those solved locally. Acts as local investigator and fixer for problems referred from Help Desk

* provides input to the change management process for relevant change requests; liaises with customers and other interested parties over implementing approved changes which will affect the range, performance, availability or ease of use of the facilities provided

* acts as the initial contact for customers for advice on how to use the IT service or rectify problems

* carries out familiarization training for new customers and following the introduction of changes to the service

* liaises with providers on which the IT service depends, such as external network services managers, operations controllers for other computer systems, premises managers and maintenance agents

* liaises with customers and management over the maintenance of an SLA which will continue to meet business needs

* maintains configuration, performance and maintenance records.

BCS ISM Cross-reference

The BCS substream Customer Service - Customer/User support is probably the closest to the role of Local Systems Administrator.

D.12 Network Services Manager

Responsibilities

The Network Services Manager has overall responsibility for the planning and on-going management of networks and network services. The **Network Services Management** module explains three subordinate roles - the Network Services Planner, the Network Services Administrator and the Network Services Controller.

Tasks

The Network Services Manager:

* estimates costs and resources for the design, implementation and operation of the network services systems and personnel, and the Network Services Management (NSM) function

* defines the roles and responsibilities of the NSM function personnel and plans their recruitment, training and development

* ensures that the Network Plan is developed and maintained by the Network Services Planner

* reviews and approves changes to the planning, design, configuration, management equipment and procedures of the network subject to change management procedures

* ensures that network services are adequately managed and administered and all relevant network management information is collected, recorded and reported

* supervises and monitors the performance of the NSM systems, personnel, procedures and hardware, including planning and scheduling, ensuring that adequate funding is available for the necessary tools

* maintains the quality of network services and instigates any remedial actions required, including

  - monitoring overall network service performance and taking action to correct deficiencies

  - monitoring and controlling the quality of individual network services

  - monitoring, controlling and reviewing security and supporting procedures

* monitors and controls the quality and cost of the network services to ensure that they are matched to business needs (within the IS strategy, service level management framework) and are within cost constraints, and produces regular reports

* ensures that all regulations and standards are enforced

* manages relationships with suppliers of network hardware, software, systems and support services, including contract negotiation, and ensures compliance to contractual commitments

* monitors the effectiveness and efficiency of the NSM function

* liaises closely with other managers within IT Services, development teams, business managers, users (via the Service Level Manager, customer liaison and Help Desk) and supplier representatives.

BCS ISM Cross-reference

See BCS model code OPN6 (Network Support substream).

D.13 Problem Manager

Responsibilities

The Problem Manager has sole responsibility for problem and error control.

Tasks

The Problem Manager:

* plans and executes a continuing publicity campaign on problem management's support of the efficient provision of quality IT services

* directs the resolution of complex problems requiring the input of multiple IT Service functions

* produces status reports covering individual problems

* produces periodic status reports identifying trends in problems

* reviews the efficiency and effectiveness of the problem management function on a periodic basis

   * develops and maintains a problem management mechanism which provides

     - support, whenever required, to Computer Operations, Network Services Control and the Help Desk to resolve incidents

     - identification of problems (ie the root cause of incidents) and subsequently their resolution or conversion to known error status

     - control of known errors and coordination of resolution activity

     - initiation of changes to systems or services to prevent the occurrence and recurrence of incidents

     - the ability to review incident and problem analysis reports to identify trends and potential problems before they occur

     - in multiple systems, an ability to take action to prevent problems in one system being replicated in others.

BCS ISM Cross-reference

See BCS model code OPB6 (Problem Management specialism substream).

D.14 Service Level Manager

Responsibilities

The Service Level Manager is responsible for both negotiating and managing the Service Level Agreements.

Tasks

The Service Level Manager:

   * creates and maintains a catalogue of all existing services offered

   * formulates, negotiates and maintains a customer/ Service Level Agreement structure

   * negotiates and agrees the initial contents, and service levels, for each SLA

   * analyzes and reviews all achieved service levels and conducts comparisons with SLAs

* produces regular reports of service achievements to customers and Senior Management

* produces forward plan of each customer's use of IT services and resources

* chairs monthly meetings with customer representatives to jointly consider the service levels

* initiates any actions necessary to improve or maintain levels of service

* prepares for and conducts regular reviews of the SLAs with the customers, and negotiates and agrees any amendments necessary.

BCS ISM Cross-reference

See BCS model cell reference USM6 (Service Level Management sub-stream).

D.15 Software Control and Distribution Manager

Responsibilities

The Software Control and Distribution (SC&D) Manager is responsible for installing and running a system to control software assets.

Tasks

The Software Control and Distribution Manager:

* mounts publicity campaigns to win support for new SC&D procedures

* plans and implements the new release building, distribution and implementation procedures

* plans and creates the Definitive Software Library (DSL) and build environments

* evaluates and procures support tools

* ensures correctness and completeness of DSL contents by controlling all inputs, outputs and housekeeping

* builds, distributes and, once tested, implements all software releases, as scheduled by the Change Advisory Board

* ensures that only authorized software is introduced into the test and live environments(s)

* assists configuration management staff to carry out configuration audits to check for the existence of unauthorized software; arranges for the removal of offending items, and takes steps to prevent recurrence of any infringements

* ensures that DSL, build and target environments and CMDB are always consistent

* continually reviews the SC&D function for efficiency and effectiveness, and future requirements.

BCS ISM Cross-reference

See BCS model OPA 4 - 6 (IS Asset Control specialism substream).

D.16 Operational Test Manager

Responsibilities

The Operational Test Manager is responsible for planning and implementing a function which can perform system, installation and acceptance testing.

Tasks

The Operational Test Manager:

* ensures all test plans and specifications are properly documented and maintained

* manages the testing function across all projects, including coordination with software development and maintenance, scheduling and resourcing

* develops procedures for running operational tests on all new and updated software and related documentation, whether developed in-house or purchased by the organization

* designs, implements and maintains test data for software as required by test plans

* produces regular management reports on test projects planned and in progress, eg establishing metrics and producing information in the areas of software quality and metrics, test team effectiveness and test team efficiency

* works with development and maintenance teams to ensure that operational test requirements are considered at the early stages of the software lifecycle

* liaises with customers, other service management functions and security officers to ensure that all are involved in the specification, execution and review of tests as appropriate

* ensures that errors are reported and that appropriate re-testing is performed

* assesses new technologies and tools which may help to automate operational testing and increase productivity

* assesses new technologies being used in development and maintenance which may have an impact on test requirements and methods

* maintains a knowledge of future demand for testing services.

BCS ISM Cross-reference

No relevant cross reference.

D.17 Supplier Manager

Responsibilities

The Supplier Manager has the key role between the IT Services Organization and external suppliers.

Tasks

The Supplier Manager:

* 'owns' the relationship on behalf of the customer organization

* is a catalyst enabling the two organizations to work together for the benefit of both

* regularly monitors the contacts between the two organizations to ensure that they are at the right level and conducted properly

* ensures that internal communications, relating to suppliers, are effective and efficient

* canvasses the views of staff within his/her organization on supplier performance and reports to senior management

* assists the Purchasing and Contracts sections in drawing up contracts with his/her supplier(s)

* is involved in the sign-off of all changes to contracts with suppliers (in many cases the Supplier Manager may well carry the final authorization for agreeing contract changes)

* is responsible for arbitrating in situations where suppliers are getting conflicting information from the customer

* is the first point of escalation for any issues or problems raised by the supplier

* visits suppliers' premises regularly to maintain visibility within that supplier

* checks invoices from suppliers to establish whether they are valid for payment (in many cases the Supplier Manager will find it more cost effective to delegate this task but must retain overall responsibility for invoice clearance).

BCS ISM Cross-reference

No relevant cross reference.

D.18 IT Services Coordinator

Responsibilities

The IT Services Coordinator has overall responsibility for ensuring the managers of IT service management functions are involved in planning processes for software development and maintenance.

Tasks

The IT Services Coordinator:

* liaises with software development and maintenance managers to identify planning requirements

* liaises with managers of service management functions to ensure that they are aware of their involvement and responsibilities in specific project plans

* participates in the selection and application of lifecycle models for infrastructure planning

* uses lifecycle models to plan for software development and maintenance

* prepares plans for the IT infrastructure required to support individual IT applications

* monitors the implementation of plans

* reports progress to senior management

* undertakes education and training of management and staff about the aims and objectives of software support.

BCS ISM Cross-reference

No relevant cross reference.

D.19 IT Security Manager

Responsibilities

The IT Security manager has security responsibilities, within the IT Services Organization, for identified areas of IT infrastructure (such as networks, computer installation, software).

Tasks

The IT Security Manager:

* coordinates IT security matters

* formulates policy as required

* produces standards, procedures and guidance as required

* carries out, acts as quality inspector, or provides advice and guidance to risk analysis reviews

* provides IT security advice and guidance as input to the planning, development and management of IT services and IT infrastructure

* provides technical input to IT security solutions based on recommendations from risk analysis reviews

* assists in the provision and maintenance of IT security awareness and training programmes

* monitors and reviews the effectiveness of IT security, and coordinates security incident reporting procedures

* liaises with other managers in IT Services, other Security Managers and the IT Security Officer responsible for IT security at the wider organizational (eg Government Department) level

* regularly reports progress through IT Services management chain.

BCS ISM Cross-reference

See BCS model cell reference ISS 3-7 (Security and Contingency Planning specialism sub-stream).

D.20 IT Services Planning and Control Manager

Responsibilities

The IT Services Planning and Control Manager is responsible for the operation of the planning, reporting and control process within the IT Services Organization.

Tasks

The IT Services Planning and Control Manager:

* implements and monitors the planning and control system within the IT Services Organization

* coordinates the production of, and facilitates the compatibility of, the IT services provision plan and IT services infrastructure plan

* produces the specification of requirements for IT services

* is custodian of the IT Services Organization's IS strategic plan

* liaises with business, IS and programme planning teams to ensure compatibility of plans

* chairs the planning and control team

* manages the administrative resource used by the planning and control function

* coordinates the production of the consolidated IT Services Organization status reports

* provides planning and control input to the IT Services Organization management team.

BCS ISM Cross-reference

No relevant cross reference.

CCTA hopes that you find this book both useful and interesting. We will welcome your comments and suggestions for improving it.
Please use this form or a photocopy, and continue on a further sheet if needed.

From:

Name

Organization

Address

Telephone

COVERAGE
Does the material cover your needs?
If not, then what additional material would you like included.

CLARITY
Are there any points which are unclear?
If yes, please detail where and why.

ACCURACY
Please give details of any inaccuracies found.

If more space is required for these or other comments, please continue overleaf.

OTHER COMMENTS

Return to: **CCTA Library**
Rosebery Court
St Andrews Business Park
NORWICH NR7 0HS

Further information

Further information on the contents of this module can be obtained from:

CCTA Library
Rosebery Court
St Andrews Business Park
NORWICH
NR7 0HS

Telephone: 01603 704 930
GTN: 3040 4930

Printed in the United Kingdom for The Stationery Office
TJ002289 8/00 C6 10170